Johnson's®

feeding
your baby

London, New York, Munich, Melbourne, Delhi

Text by Tracey Godridge
For Cora, Eden, and Noah

Senior editor Julia North
U.S. senior editor Jennifer Williams
Senior art editors Glenda Fisher, Hannah Moore
Project editor Angela Baynham
Project art editor Alison Tumer
DTP designer Karen Constanti
Production controller Heather Hughes
Managing editor Anna Davidson
Managing art editor Emma Forge
Photography art direction Sally Smallwood
Photography Ruth Jenkinson
Americanizer Christine Heilman
Proofreader John Searcy

Category publisher Corinne Roberts
First American Edition, 2004

Published in the United States by
DK Publishing, Inc., 375 Hudson Street,
New York, New York 10014

04 05 06 07 08 10 9 8 7 6 5 4 3 2 1

A Cataloging-in-Publication record for this book is available from the Library of Congress.

ISBN 0-7566-0352-8

Reproduced by Colourscan, Singapore
Printed in Italy by Graphicom

Discover more at
www.dk.com

A message to parents from

Johnson's®

The most precious gift in the world is a new baby. To your little one, you are the center of the universe. And by following your most basic instincts to touch, hold, and talk to your baby, you provide the best start to a happy, healthy life.

Our baby products encourage parents to care for and nurture their children through the importance of touch, developing a deep, loving bond that transcends all others.

Parenting is not an exact science, nor is it a one-size-fits-all formula. For more than a hundred years, Johnson & Johnson has supported the healthcare needs of parents and healthcare professionals, and we understand that all parents feel more confident in their role when they have information they can trust.

That is why we offer this book as our commitment to you to provide scientifically sound, professionally reviewed guidance on the important topics of pregnancy, babycare and child development.

As you read through this book, the most important thing to remember is this: you know your baby better than anyone else. By watching, listening, and having confidence in your natural ability, you will know how to use the information you have in your hands, for the benefit of the baby in your arms.

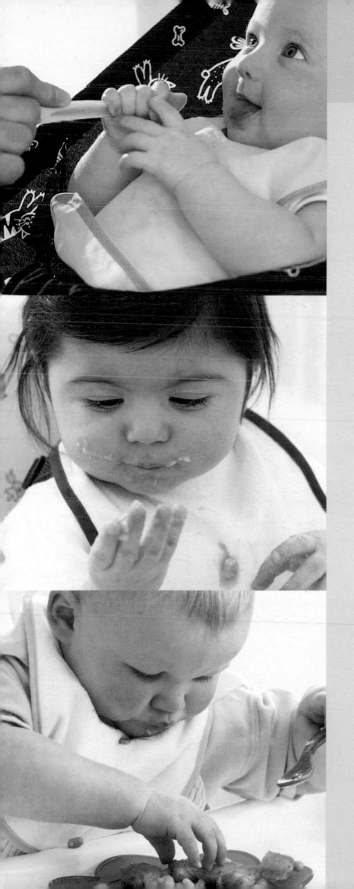

Contents

1 Getting ready for solids **6**

2 First tastes **12**

3 Around 6 months **22**

4 7 to 9 months **30**

5 9 to 12 months **38**

6 One year and up **46**

7 Happy, healthy eating **52**

Weaning chart **60**

Useful contacts **62**

Index **63**

Acknowledgments **64**

" I love breastfeeding Eve. I'm also **excited** about giving her some solid food. She already enjoys **sitting with us** at mealtimes. "

LIZ, mother of five-month-old Eve

1

Getting ready for solids

Breast milk is the perfect food for your baby during her first year. But as she grows, milk alone is no longer enough. For healthy physical development, your baby needs to learn how to eat solid food. This is also the first step toward feeding herself and joining in family meals.

Why does your baby need solid food?

As your baby gets bigger, she needs more calories to maintain her growth. If she stays on a diet of breast milk , she'll have to feed more often and her needs will not be satisfied.

Solid food can give your baby the extra calories she needs without filling her up too quickly. It can also give her the extra nutrients her body now requires. For example, from six months, your baby's natural supply of iron is starting to dwindle. Iron is vital for healthy growth, and breast milk cannot provide her with enough.

Introducing your baby to solids is also her first step toward enjoying healthy food and discovering that sharing meals is fun. Your baby is becoming more independent—she is learning how to sit up unaided and to grab what she wants; she loves to put things in her mouth, and she wants to be included in everything.

Learning how to eat solid food and joining in family meals is the next step on her journey to independence.

When to start

The recommended age to start getting your baby used to solids has traditionally been between four and six months. However, experts now believe that babies need nothing more than breast milk for the first six months of their lives. If your baby seems dissatisfied after her usual milk feeding and is less than six months old, try breastfeeding more often, or talk to your healthcare provider. Whether you are breastfeeding or bottle-feeding formula, weaning should start at around six months.

In order for your baby to accept, swallow, and digest solid food, certain physical developments need to occur:
- loss of the tongue-thrust reflex – at birth your baby naturally pushes anything that goes into her mouth

out again with her tongue, but between four and six months this reflex disappears
- development of her jaw and tongue so she can move food to the back of her mouth to swallow
- development of coordination and head control so she can maintain the posture needed for swallowing
- maturity of the gastrointestinal tract so she can digest different foods
- the ability to cope with a larger volume of food in her stomach.

Checklist

Your baby needs to start eating solid food because:

- milk alone can no longer satisfy her physical needs

- her stores of iron are running out and she needs an additional source

- eating solid food is fun—and your baby wants to be part of the family!

Is my baby ready for solids?

Your baby will be ready for solids some time around six months of age. There is no hard and fast rule—as with other skills, such as sitting up or crawling, some babies are ready to move on earlier than others. The deciding factor should be your own baby's needs and development. If you are unsure, talk to your healthcare provider.

Don't start too soon

Until the age of six months, all your baby's nutritional needs are met by your breast milk. Between the ages of four and six months, your baby loses her natural tongue–thrust reflex (see page 7), and as her digestive system matures, she will become able to cope with solid food—waiting until six months is especially important if you have a family history of allergies. Once she is approaching this age, start to watch out for the following signs:

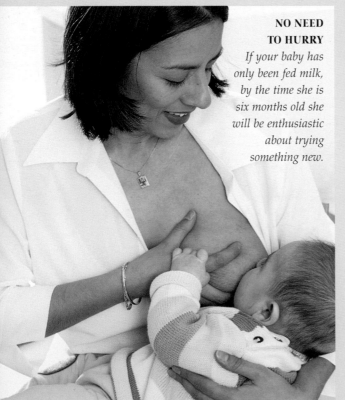

NO NEED TO HURRY
If your baby has only been fed milk, by the time she is six months old she will be enthusiastic about trying something new.

★ **She seems more hungry than usual**
When your baby starts shortening the length of time between feedings or even starts waking in the night for an extra feeding, chances are she could be ready to give solids a try.

★ **She can hold her head up well**
Your baby needs good head control before she can safely be given puréed foods; otherwise, there is a risk of choking. By now, she should be able to lift her head properly when she is propped up or strapped into a reclining chair.

★ **She's interested in the food you eat**
Watch your baby at the table. Is she following each bite you take? Does she look as if she's imitating your chewing? Does she make noises and wave her hands as if saying, "Hey, can I have some?" By six months, most babies are expressing a desire for solid food.

What about premature babies?

If your baby was born early, you need to be careful when calculating her age for starting solids. Avoid introducing them until at least four to six months after her due date rather than after her birthday.

Delaying the introduction of solids much beyond six months may cause problems later on, since teaching older babies to chew can be difficult. In addition, your baby may not be getting all the nutrients she needs from milk alone after this time. Consult your healthcare provider about when to start if you are unsure.

Once you feel your baby is ready to start solids, it's important to go at her pace. Your baby will—like all other babies—discover how to lift her head, swallow purée, and eventually hold her own spoon and feed herself. But she is also unique and will do these things only when she is ready.

Your baby still needs milk

Your baby is not ready to give up the breast or bottle just because she starts eating solid food. To begin with, she'll simply be getting used to new tastes and textures, and much of what you put in her mouth will come straight back out, so she

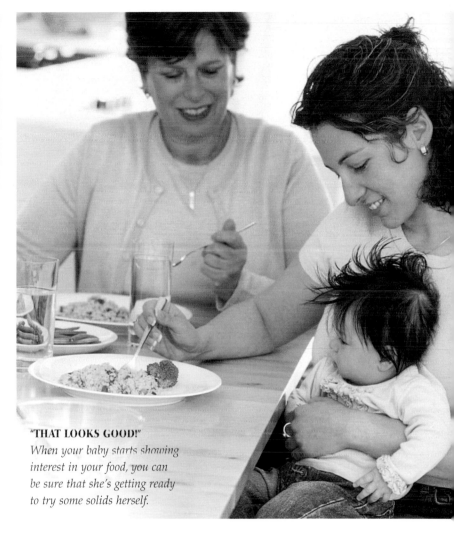

"THAT LOOKS GOOD!"
When your baby starts showing interest in your food, you can be sure that she's getting ready to try some solids herself.

Ben, my eldest, was a hungry baby. Within a few weeks of starting solids, he was devouring everything in sight. Thomas was more laid-back and took longer to get going—but now he loves mealtimes as much as his brother does.

JAN, mother of Ben, 5, and Thomas, 3

still needs her full supply of breast milk or formula. In fact, this will be an important source of nutrition for her until she is one year old.

Experiencing solids

For your baby, tasting solids for the first time is an incredible experience. When you offer her these first tastes, you are doing a lot more than just giving her the nourishment she needs—you are stimulating her senses in a way she has never experienced before.

HEAD CONTROL
Your baby's ability to hold his head up without support is a key sign that you will be able to start feeding him solid food before long.

● Taste

From an early age, "tasting" is a way of exploring, and as soon as your baby is able, everything within reach will be put in her mouth—although she may not always like the taste! She was born with a full set of 10,000 taste buds and, while they take some years to mature fully, she can already tell the difference between sweet and sour.

● Smell

Just as babies prefer sweet tastes, they also prefer sweet smells such as vanilla and banana. In fact, your baby's sense of smell is so acute that she is able to tell the difference between your breast milk and that of another mother. Smelling is another way in which your baby learns about the world around her—and giving her new foods offers her the chance to discover new smells.

● Touch

Feeling things with her mouth is one of the most important ways your baby has of exploring and learning about her environment. And food teaches her a lot about texture— it can be soft (mashed banana) or hard (a cube of cheese), rough (a rice cracker) or smooth (a grape). Even a runny purée feels strangely different to your baby's mouth compared with milk.

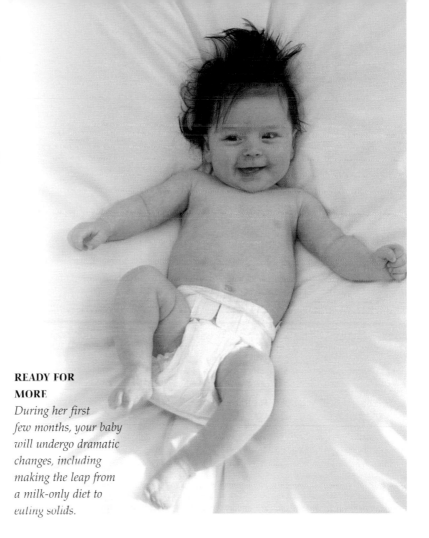

READY FOR MORE
During her first few months, your baby will undergo dramatic changes, including making the leap from a milk-only diet to eating solids.

Questions & Answers

Members of my family suffer from asthma and eczema. Does this affect when I give my baby solids?
Your baby is more likely to be prone to allergies if they run in the family, so it's best to be cautious (see pages 54–55). Waiting until your baby is at least six months old before introducing solids can help prevent allergies from occurring.

How are allergies caused?
While your baby is young, her gut is more porous, so proteins (the parts of food that cause allergies) can leak into the bloodstream. Your baby's immune system reacts to these proteins in the way it would react to germs. Then, whenever she eats that particular food, her immune system reacts as if it is an infection. She has what is called an "allergic reaction."

Why does it help to wait until six months before introducing solids?
The older your baby is when she first tastes real food, the more mature her digestive system has become. The proteins are less likely to leak into the bloodstream and your baby can handle different foods without having an allergic reaction. Also, her immune system is more mature and better at recognizing the difference between a food protein and bacteria. Exclusively breastfeeding until your baby is six months old may not stop her from developing an allergy, but it can reduce the likelihood and severity. In babies who have no solids before six months, allergies appear later, tend to be milder, and the children grow out of them earlier.

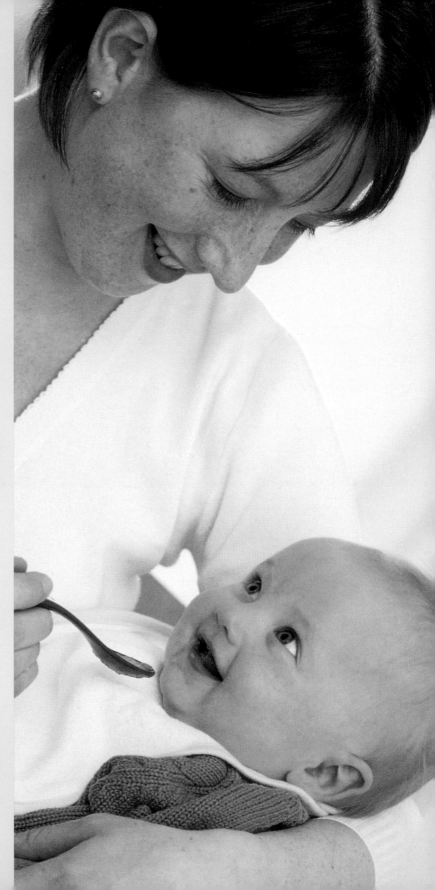

" I'll **never forget** the first time I gave James baby rice cereal— my husband took a **memorable photo** of him smiling at me as he had his first taste of solid food. "

RUTH, mother of six-month-old James

First tastes

Giving your baby his first taste of solid food is an exciting moment. But his first tastes are more about experiencing something new than gaining extra nourishment. Being prepared—knowing which foods to serve and what to expect—will help the moment go smoothly. Here, we look at what you will need and how you can make your baby's first experience of solid food a happy one.

Be prepared

Your baby's first taste of food is a major milestone in his development and one you need to be ready for. Once you decide that the right time to introduce solids is approaching, it's worth preparing for the big moment so you can feel calm and in control as you offer your baby his first mouthfuls.

You'll need to make a trip to the store to buy your first few items of baby food. But don't go overboard. Remember, at this stage you are just offering your baby his first tastes of solid food, and it may be a while yet before he's eating three meals a day.

What you will need

For preparing food, you will need:
• a nylon chopping board (wooden boards can harbor germs)
• one of the following for puréeing food, depending on budget: a nylon or steel sieve and a plastic and nylon or stainless steel spoon; a hand-turned food mill; or a small hand-held electric blender or food processor
• a steamer—good for fast cooking to preserve nutrients
• plastic containers with airtight lids for storing food in the refrigerator
• ice-cube trays for freezing surplus food in convenient small portions
• freezer bags for storing frozen cubes of purée.

For serving food, you will need:
• lots of soft fabric bibs (easy to wear and easy to wash) and a plastic bib with a curved bottom designed to catch food (especially useful once your baby starts feeding himself)
• a set of plastic bowls—unbreakable and easy to wash
• plastic teaspoons with soft or round edges—easier on tender gums.

Where should my baby sit?

You can sit your baby on your lap or strap him into his baby seat or car seat, preferably placed on the floor for safety. If he still can't sit up unaided, he will need to be slightly reclined—but he should be upright enough to eat and swallow without choking.

Great expectations

Lots of parents have a camera ready to record the moment when their baby has his first taste of solid food—but don't expect too much! Remember that this is the first time your baby has tasted anything other than milk. (continued on page 16)

Which are the best first foods for my baby?

Until now, your baby has tasted food only from the breast or bottle, so to begin with, the best foods are those that are most like breast milk or formula. He'll be happiest if the food you offer has a bland, milky taste and a runny consistency so he can easily suck from the spoon. His digestive system is still immature, so these first foods should be gentle on his stomach, too.

Baby rice cereal

Most babies start with specially made baby rice cereal. It has many benefits:
★ it only needs mixing with breast milk or formula or a little cooled boiled water
★ it can be easily thinned to a texture not much thicker than milk
★ it can be easily digested
★ it is unlikely to trigger an allergic reaction because it is gluten-free (see pages 28–29)

baby rice cereal

pear

carrots

Baby rice cereal is enriched with iron, reserves of which may be running short.

Pears can be stewed, then puréed, and are rich in vitamin C.

Puréed carrots are popular—they have a sweeter taste than green vegetables.

★ it is enriched with iron that can be easily absorbed (exclusively breastfed babies in particular might be needing an extra boost of this—see page 7)

★ it tastes reasonably familiar with the addition of breast milk or formula.

Fruit and vegetable purées

Fruit and vegetable purées may taste more unusual than cereals, but many babies seem to prefer them to baby rice cereal. They are also unlikely to cause an allergic reaction. It's a good idea to try vegetable purées before fruit purées because your baby will naturally like sweeter tastes best, so if you start with fruit, you may find that he tends to refuse less sweet foods.

Try carrots, potatoes, sweet potatoes, parsnips, rutabagas, stewed pears or apples, bananas, melons, and mangoes. Avoid giving all yellow or orange vegetables, because this can cause some babies to take on a yellow/orange color.

Getting the texture right

First solid foods are not solid at all—in fact, they need to be semi-liquid and as much like milk in consistency as possible so they are easy to swallow. You can prepare baby rice cereal with cooled boiled water, but breast milk or formula will give it a familiar taste and make it more acceptable to your baby. Purées of fruits and vegetables will also need to be thinned down using cooled boiled water, breast milk, or formula.

bananas   potatoes   sweet potatoes

Bananas are simple to prepare—just mash them. They are also easy to digest.

Puréed potatoes are a popular first food, since babies like the bland taste.

Sweet potatoes, like carrots, are often more palatable to babies than green vegetables.

(continued from page 13)

The new taste and texture will probably baffle him, and chances are, what goes in—if anything does—will roll right back out again!

Learning to eat food takes time and practice. Your baby will go at his own pace, but there is plenty you can do to encourage his interest in food.

• Let him sit on your lap at family meals so he can see everyone enjoying their food.

• As he becomes more adept at using his hands, he'll love playing with his food. Let him squish a piece of cooked pasta or dip his hands in some yogurt.

• Talk to him while you are preparing his food—whether you are getting ready to breastfeed, fixing a bottle, or getting his solids ready.

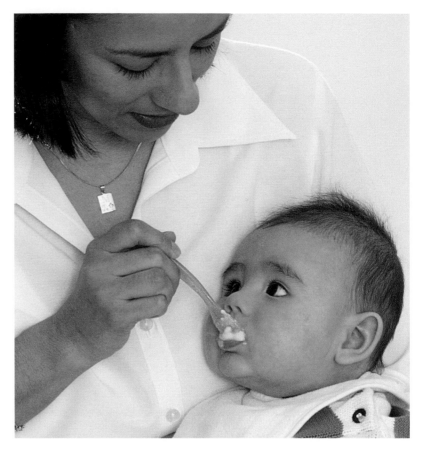

How to give the first feeding

• Talking to your baby the whole time, prepare a small amount of food using the methods described on page 20. Then give him up to half of his usual milk feeding to take the edge off his appetite.

• Sit him on your lap or in a baby seat or car seat. Using a plastic spoon, place a tiny amount of food in between his lips. Don't push it in too far or your baby may gag. And don't worry if he pushes it right back out—he'll soon learn how to suck food from the spoon. A tiny amount will stay in his mouth, and you can scoop the remainder up and slip it back in.

• Give your baby lots of loving attention—chat, smile, tell him how wonderful he is. Make a point of touching him

and stroking him whenever you can to help him feel safe and secure.

• Try another spoonful, but don't expect him to take more than a couple of tiny teaspoons. Don't worry if most of it ends up smeared around his face—he's discovering what it feels like and is more likely to let you try again if he is having fun.

• Once your baby has had enough, he'll turn his head away, close his mouth, or lean back.

• Tell him how good he is and give him lots of cuddles. Finish up with the remainder of his milk feed if he's interested.

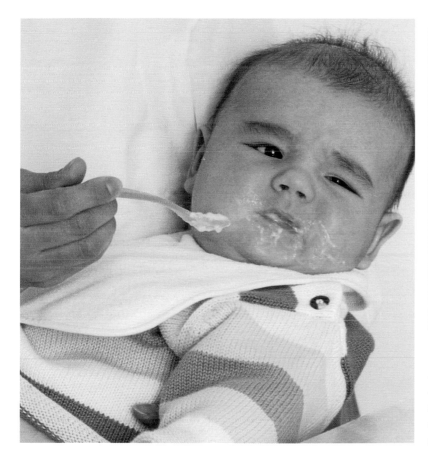

Expert tip

It's not unusual for a baby to gag if he is offered a food he doesn't recognize, too large a mouthful, or a texture that's slightly thicker than normal. Gagging is a protective reflex; it helps get the food back to the front of the mouth where it can be spat out or repositioned. Try thinning the food a little more if your baby gags. All food, however, can cause choking, so it's vital never to leave your baby alone while he has food or drink in his mouth. Talk to your healthcare provider if gagging or choking become a regular occurrence.

A WHOLE NEW EXPERIENCE
At first, give your baby only tiny amounts of food at a time. When he has had enough, he will close his mouth and turn his head away.

Tell him what you are doing and praise him for watching. He'll love your attention and learn to associate mealtimes with happy occasions.

A new skill to learn

Once you've decided that today is the day for giving your baby a taste of something new, get everything ready beforehand and choose a time when you are both feeling happy and relaxed. Introducing new foods takes time, so it may be worth putting on the answering machine and forgetting about other chores while you give your baby your full attention.

Most babies make faces from surprise no matter how much they like the new tastes. So how do you know whether your baby loves or loathes the food you are giving him?

• If he likes it, he'll open his mouth for more, in which case you can continue to offer him a few teaspoons each day, gradually increasing the thickness of the purées.

• If he doesn't like it, he'll turn his head away, cry, or seem uninterested.

Don't worry—chances are today is just not the day. Try again tomorrow. If your baby still isn't eager, wait a few days and give it another try. If he's still not interested, talk to your healthcare provider.

Don't be worried if your baby is finding it hard to get the hang of eating solid food—until now he has always taken his food by sucking, and learning how to feed from a spoon needs lots of practice. His tongue-thrust reflex (see page 7) is only just starting to disappear and

Trying new tastes

Some babies are naturally reluctant to try new tastes. Here are some ideas to help you both.

- Serve your baby's food at room temperature or slightly warmed.

- If your baby rejects the spoon, dip a clean finger into the food and let him suck the food from it.

- Try offering some food after a shorter breast- or bottle-feed than usual. If he's alert but not over-hungry, he may be more eager.

- Don't prepare too much—one advantage of ready-to-mix baby rice cereal is that it provides tiny servings without wasting food.

often the food you give your baby will simply dribble out because he doesn't know how to get it far enough back on his tongue to swallow.

Give him only a tiny bit of food, holding the spoon close to his lips. If he likes what he tastes, he'll soon discover that by sucking he can draw the food off the spoon. Sucking will also help him get the food to the back of his mouth so he can swallow it.

When your baby has had enough, he'll close his mouth or turn his head away. No matter how much is left in his bowl, don't force him to eat any more—your baby needs to decide for himself whether he's still hungry and which foods he likes. And while,

at this stage, it's hard to tell whether he's rejecting a new taste because he doesn't like it or is still mastering the art of eating, it's better to be cautious than pushy.

What to avoid

Never add any of the following to your baby's food:

- salt—this can overload his kidneys

- sugar—this can encourage a sweet tooth

- honey, in liquid or solid form—it can contain spores that cause infant botulism: the digestive systems of babies under one year old are immature, and the spores can grow there and cause life-threatening illness.

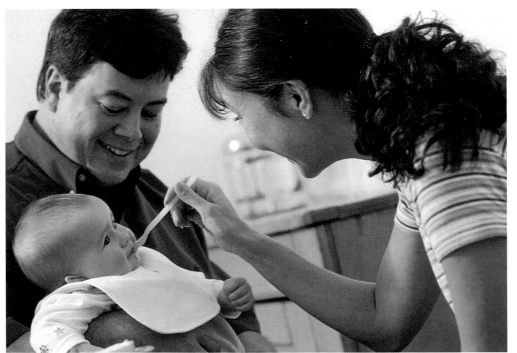

DAD'S TURN
Starting on solids provides a great opportunity for dad to get involved with feeding.

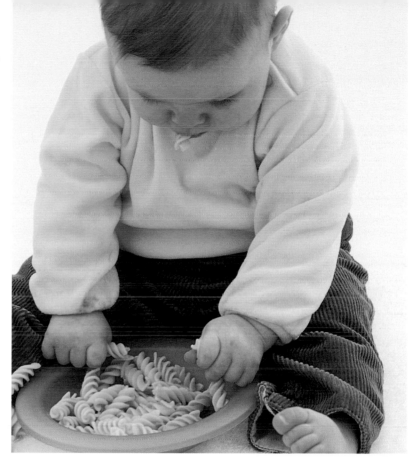

PASTA PLAY
Allowing your baby to handle solid food will help him explore and get used to different shapes and textures

Don't be tempted to mix baby rice cereal into your baby's bottle. Adding cereal to bottles risks overfeeding your baby and can cause choking. Also, it's important that your baby gets used to the mechanics of eating: taking a spoonful, resting, taking another, and stopping when he's full. Experiencing his first foods in this way will help your child develop good eating habits that will last a lifetime.

Diaper changes

Once your baby starts eating solids, you will notice changes in the consistency and color of his stools. They will be more solid, darker, and probably smellier! This may come as a bit of a shock—especially if up until now your baby has been totally breastfed and his diapers fairly inoffensive. The change is perfectly normal. His digestive system is still immature and the food often doesn't change much in between going in and coming out again.

If your baby's stools become hard, you notice him straining, or he passes fewer stools per day, talk to your healthcare provider—your baby may be constipated.

Questions & Answers

When's the best time of day to give my baby his first foods?
Your baby needs to be relaxed, not too hungry, and not too tired. Early morning and late evening may not be the best times, since your baby might be hungry, half awake, or half asleep. He may be more cooperative midmorning and in late afternoon. Watch him closely and feed him when he's happy, hasn't had a milk feeding for a while, but isn't too hungry.

Will starting my baby on solid food help him to sleep through the night?
Lots of parents imagine that introducing their babies to solids will help them sleep through the night. Research shows that this isn't the case. Babies routinely wake in the night—even when they are not hungry—and until they learn how to comfort themselves and fall back to sleep on their own, they are unable to sleep for extended periods of time.

My baby just isn't interested in solids. What should I do?
It's much more important at this stage that both of you enjoy mealtimes, and if, despite your best efforts, your baby isn't eager to give solids a try, don't force the issue. Instead, go back to breast- or bottle-feeding for a few days, then try again. If you have concerns, talk to your healthcare provider.

How should I prepare my baby's food?

Preparing simple purées made from fruits and vegetables for your baby doesn't take long—and it's less expensive than store-bought baby food. With a few simple precautions and cooking tips, you can give your baby safe and healthy meals. You can also easily prepare small quantities in advance so they are ready when your baby needs to be fed.

Making your own purées

Try to cook fresh fruit and vegetables within a day or so of buying them.

1 Wash and prepare the fruit or vegetable and cut into even-sized pieces.

2 Steam or boil (use as little water as possible to preserve the nutrients).

3 When soft, allow the food to cool a little, then purée it using a hand mill, food processor, or hand-held blender. Alternatively, you can push it through a sieve.

4 Test the temperature of the food on your fingertip or arm before giving it to your baby—room temperature or slightly warm is best. Babies' palates are very sensitive, so be careful not to burn your baby's mouth.

HEALTHY COOKING
Using a steamer to cook your baby's food will help preserve the nutrients that are normally lost during the cooking process.

PURÉEING YOUR BABY'S FOOD
A hand-operated food mill is ideal for puréeing your baby's cooked food. This stage won't last for long, so don't buy an electric blender just for this purpose.

PREPARE IN ADVANCE
You can have home-cooked baby food always on hand if you make a large quantity of purée in advance and freeze spoonfuls of it in a sterilized ice-cube tray.

Freezing and storing

At this stage, your baby is only tasting a tiny amount of food. Unused purée can be spooned into a sterilized ice-cube tray and frozen until needed. You can also freeze ahead—make a large amount of purée, spoon it into a sterilized ice-cube tray, and freeze until the cubes are solid. Dump the cubes into a plastic bag, seal, and label before returning to the freezer. Individual cubes can then be removed and defrosted in the refrigerator in a bowl or on a plate. Heat thoroughly as and when required.

You can sterilize a freshly washed ice-cube tray by washing it in the dishwasher or putting it in a pan of boiling water for 5 to 10 minutes.

Food hygiene

Food poisoning is easy to prevent. Make eating safe for your baby by taking the following precautions:
★ wash your hands carefully before feeding your baby—especially if you have been handling raw food

HANDY NUTRITION
When frozen, take the cubes of puréed food out of the tray and store in sealed freezer bags, one type of food per bag. Carefully label and date each bag and use within three months of freezing.

★ keep kitchen equipment and work spaces as clean as possible
★ don't save leftovers from the bowl your baby has just used—bacteria will grow and any enzymes from your baby's saliva will thin the food out
★ if you are using a ready-made jar of food, remove as much as you need rather than feeding directly from the jar, unless you are finishing the jar off
★ if you are heating your baby's food, heat only enough for one meal and discard any leftovers
★ refrigerate cold food for no more than 24 hours, and use warm food as soon as it's ready.

" Bethany turned her nose up at baby rice cereal but she **seems to like** puréed carrots. Next week, I'll try some **new vegetables**. I don't want her to get bored! "

DEBBIE, mother of Bethany, six months

3

Around 6 months

Some time around her six-month birthday, you can give your baby her first taste of solid food. She may start on baby rice cereal or puréed carrots. If she likes it, you can start to introduce new foods and food combinations, helping her build up to two or three mini-meals a day. Don't expect too much too soon—your baby will take time to adjust to her new eating routine.

A happy routine

If your baby loves her first tastes, over the next few weeks you can start introducing a wider variety, but it's important to take your time, and watch out for allergic reactions.

Keep to the same routine each time you offer your baby some food. Establishing consistent, predictable mealtimes at this early age will help your baby become aware of what is happening—and what is expected of her. Always chat to her about what you are doing, talk about the food and utensils, smile, and tell her how well she is doing.

Introducing new foods

For a healthy diet, your baby ideally needs to eat as wide a range of foods as possible. Once she is eating two or three spoonfuls of baby cereal or a homemade purée such as carrot every day, try a different single food. Don't be worried if she doesn't accept it right away. It's perfectly normal to have to offer a new food between 10 and 20 times before it's accepted. Once your baby clearly likes the taste, give this new food exclusively for at least a couple of days before trying another.

Offering one food at a time, and only one new food every two or three days, has two advantages:

- your baby can get used to each new taste and texture
- if there are any signs of an allergic reaction—such as a stomachache, diarrhea, or rashes—you will more readily identify which food was the culprit.

First purées (see pages 14–15) to try include:

- **vegetables:** carrots, parsnips, rutabagas, potatoes, sweet potatoes

Expert tip

The number of "meals" your baby will have each day depends on your baby. To begin with, solid food is just an addition to her diet and not a replacement for the breast milk or formula she needs. If after a few days she's just managing a couple of teaspoons once a day, that's fine. If she gives you the impression she'd like more, you can offer her the same size serving twice or even three times a day.

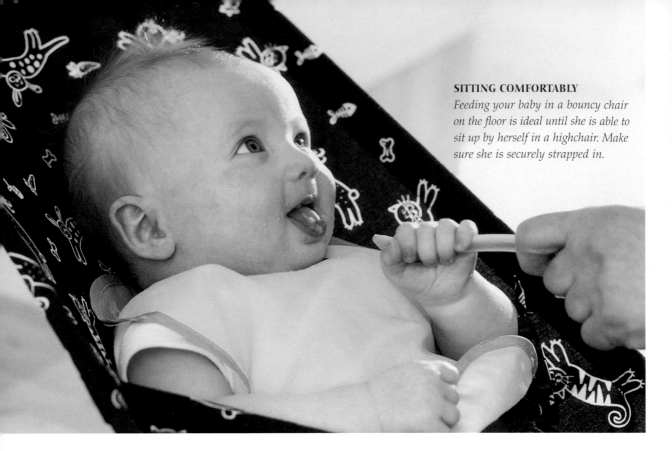

> "*I always prepare Daniel's purée before I breastfeed him. He loves sitting in his chair watching me. I'm sure he's finishing on the breast quicker so he can get to his solid food sooner!*"

SIMONE, mother of Daniel, six months

- fruit: cooked apples, cooked pears, mashed bananas, mangoes, melons, peaches, avocados.

Once your baby is happy taking semi-liquid food from a spoon, gradually start to thicken the purée or cereal by adding less liquid. This allows your baby to practice her chewing (gumming) and swallowing skills and will help ease the transition from purées to lumpier food.

If your baby has a reaction

Although some foods are more likely than others to cause problems, any food can potentially trigger an allergic reaction. Food allergies that affect the immune system are rare, but some children find certain foods more difficult to tolerate than others and may have a reaction.

If you think your baby had a reaction to a particular food, wait a couple of weeks before trying it again. The same reaction two or three times would suggest that your baby is sensitive and you should wait a few months before reintroducing it. Most babies eventually grow out of this kind of food problem. Consult your healthcare provider if you are unsure.

Food combinations

Once your baby has eaten several single foods with no adverse reaction, you can start mixing two foods together. Don't be tempted to try mixing one food your baby loves with another she hates, or she may end up hating both. Combinations that work well at this age include:

- broccoli and sweet potatoes
- carrots and parsnips
- potatoes and parsnips
- stewed apples and pears
- bananas and mangoes
- melons and peaches.

Does she like it?

Sometimes it can be difficult to tell from your baby's reaction whether or not she likes a new food. Sweet foods such as mashed bananas or stewed apples are usually accepted with a look of real pleasure. But if your baby makes faces or even appears to wince, this doesn't necessarily mean she doesn't like what she's eating.

Remember, every new taste will be unfamiliar if a baby's only experience of food up until now has been milk. Your baby's facial expression may just be a reaction to the new taste or texture. Offer her another taste—if she opens her mouth, she obviously wants to try it again. If she turns her head away, don't persist, but don't give up altogether, either. Try it again a few

Milk needs

Once your baby is happily taking two or three solid "meals" a day with milk in between (even if the "meals" consist of only a couple of spoonfuls at each serving), you may find that she's not feeding as much from the breast or bottle. Usually, early morning and pre-bedtime feedings stay the same, but during the day your baby may nurse a little less or take a little less formula.

- **Good for nutrition** Although your baby is starting to eat real food, milk is still an essential part of her diet. Purées offer little in the way of extra calories—and calories are what your baby needs to maintain her growth and

weight gain. Until she eats three proper meals a day, she still needs around 20 fl oz (600ml) of milk a day. If you are breastfeeding, it's impossible to check, but if you let your baby take the lead, chances are she's taking what she needs. If you have concerns, talk to your healthcare provider.

- **Good for comfort** Although your baby is starting to recognize that solids can satisfy hunger as well as milk, sucking is still a way of feeling close to you. Your baby loves nothing better than feeling safe and secure in your arms, and breastfeeding or bottle-feeding her is still important as a way of giving her comfort.

Stomach complaints

- If your baby becomes constipated, avoid baby cereals for a while and offer her fruit or vegetable purées and plenty of fluids such as breast milk, formula, or cooled boiled water.

- If your baby has a bout of diarrhea, avoid the food she last had for a while—it may be that her digestive system cannot yet handle that particular food. Try it again in a few weeks.

- Changes in diet may cause upsets to your baby's stomach. Speak to your healthcare provider if you have any worries about your baby's reaction to food.

days later—but don't look anxious or concerned when you offer it. You don't want to unconsciously influence your baby's reaction.

Your baby's appetite

It's normal for your baby's appetite to vary from day to day. One day she'll amaze you with how much she eats and the next day she will frustrate you because she won't want a thing!

Changes in appetite can be caused by lots of different factors, including a growth spurt, how tired or alert your baby feels, whether she's sick, and even the weather. The cold, for example, makes food taste different, and so can feeling cranky. For these

reasons, the foods that she loved yesterday may today be less appealing. It's also natural for your baby to develop preferences—for example, some children, because of genetic influences, are more able to distinguish bitter taste; some prefer strong flavors, others sweet.

Developing good habits

Encouraging your baby to develop good eating habits now will have a positive effect on her health and well-being throughout her life.

- Getting her used to lots of different tastes now will help her enjoy a varied diet later—once she's eaten a new food for two or three days without difficulty, introduce another.

Questions & Answers

My baby will eat only puréed fruit. How can I encourage her to try vegetable purées?
Babies often show a dislike for food that isn't sweet. This is because they are used to breast milk or formula, both of which are quite sweet. Try thinning a vegetable purée with her usual milk—this may encourage her to give it a try. She may also find carrots and sweet potatoes more palatable than green vegetables.

By the time she's finished breast-feeding, my baby isn't hungry. How can I improve her appetite?

Your baby is probably too full after her milk to bother with solid food. Cut down on the amount of breast milk she has before eating solids—just give her enough to take the edge off her appetite. Then offer her the remainder of her feeding after her solids.

My baby doesn't appear to swallow anything—most of what I put in her mouth comes right back out again! What can I do about this?
If your baby consistently pushes her food out with her tongue so it dribbles down her chin, it may be too thick for her to handle. Remember, until now she's only had food the consistency of water. Try

diluting her food more—and use a bib to help save on the laundry.

My baby often cries for her food—and then keeps on crying between mouthfuls. Why does she do this?
Your baby is used to sucking when she's hungry—and it will take her a while before she realizes that solid food will satisfy her in the way that milk does. If she takes the food willingly but continues to cry while eating, this doesn't necessarily mean she doesn't like what you are giving her—it may just mean that she's still hungry.

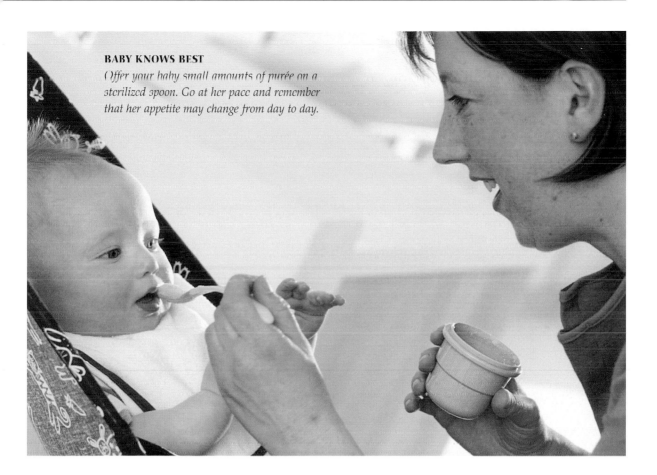

BABY KNOWS BEST
Offer your baby small amounts of purée on a sterilized spoon. Go at her pace and remember that her appetite may change from day to day.

- Avoid adding sugar or salt to her food—not only are they bad for her health in general, but salt can damage her kidneys. Also, once children get used to these tastes, food that's less seasoned can seem bland. You can use a tiny amount of herbs for seasoning.
- Give your baby lots of attention at mealtimes—talk to her, stroke her hair, and praise her for eating well.
- Encourage your baby to join in—she's a long way from being able to feed herself, but she'll enjoy having her own spoon to wave around.

- Make feeding a family affair—moving on to solids is a great way for dad to get involved too, especially if until now you have only breastfed.

Messy eaters

Even though you have control over the spoon, don't expect to keep your baby—or your kitchen—spotless. First foods are as much about experimenting as nourishment—and your baby will be desperate to get her hands on the spoon and the dish. Your baby needs lots of positive attention, so it's best to try to ignore the inevitable mess by:
- keeping lots of kitchen towels on hand for wiping up
- always putting a washable bib on your baby before each mealtime
- spreading a mat or newspaper on the floor under her baby chair
- keeping a garbage bag nearby.

Store-bought baby food

There are many advantages to making your own baby food—it's cheap, easy, and your baby can get

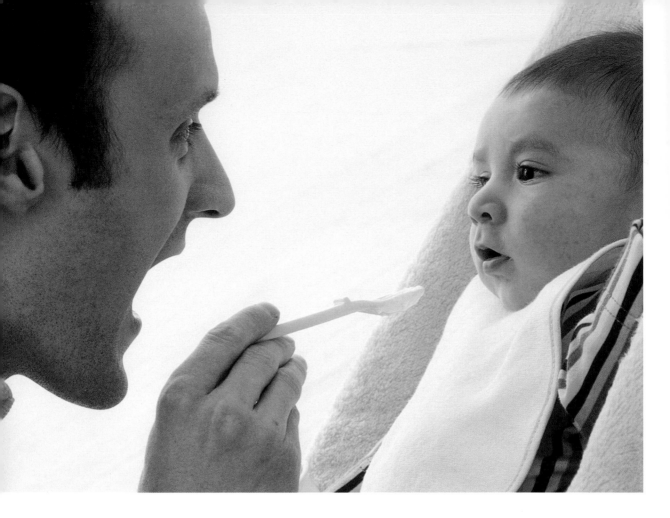

What is gluten?

Gluten is a protein found in wheat, barley, rye, and perhaps oats. Sensitivity to gluten can trigger celiac disease (see page 54). In a small number of babies, when the intestine comes in contact with gluten, an allergic reaction occurs and the intestine's lining becomes smooth, preventing nutrients from being properly absorbed, and this is associated with permanent intolerance to gluten. Symptoms include stomach pain, diarrhea, weight loss, irritability, and nausea.

Foods that contain gluten, such as bread, pasta, and crackers, should never be given to babies under six months. Once your baby is six months old, her intestines are less likely to develop gluten intolerance.

If celiac disease is diagnosed, your child will need to eat a gluten-free diet for life. She'll be referred to a dietician who can advise you what she can and can't eat. Nowadays, larger supermarkets stock gluten-free alternatives, including bread, biscuits, cereals, and pasta.

WATCH AND LEARN
Open your mouth as you offer your baby her food, and she will probably open hers in response.

used to the types of food your family normally eats. But there are times when ready-made jars are more convenient—for example, when you are traveling.

You can choose from many different flavors and ingredients, and the foods are usually categorized according to age. They don't contain salt but some do have added sugar and modified starch, so it's worth reading the list of ingredients carefully.

When using commercially made baby food, keep your baby safe by following these guides:

- check the expiration date on the container
- store unopened jars in a cool place
- make sure the vacuum seal button is down—don't use a jar if the seal has popped up
- don't feed from the jar—take the amount of food your baby needs out of the jar and serve separately
- once opened, keep the jar with its contents in the refrigerator—it should stay fresh for one to two days, but always read the label.

Are organic fruits and vegetables best?

Many people worry about the effects on children's health of pesticides and other chemicals used to produce food. Organic fruits and vegetables are grown in soil fertilized with manure and compost instead of synthetic chemicals. Research has shown, however, that levels of pesticides in fruits and vegetables are typically well below the safety levels set by government agencies. You can take extra care with your child's health by washing fruits and vegetables thoroughly before cooking and serving.

Foods to avoid

Advice on which foods are suitable for your baby can sometimes change, so check also with your healthcare provider. But as a general guideline, you should not give the following foods to babies who are six months old.

- **nuts and nut products,** especially those containing peanuts: for babies with a family history of allergies, continue to avoid these up to the age of three; whole nuts should not be given to children until age seven or older because of the risk of choking

- **foods that carry a higher risk of food poisoning,** such as mold-ripened cheeses, liver pâté, and soft-boiled eggs (up to the age of nine months, only egg yolk should be given, since this is the high-nutrition part of the egg, and whites are more likely to cause allergies)

- **salt:** your baby's kidneys are too immature to cope with this

- **sugar, honey, or other sweeteners:** can lead to a sweet tooth and honey can also contain a potentially dangerous spore (see page 18)—if you need to, sweeten desserts with mashed bananas

- **soft drinks:** may contain high levels of artificial sweeteners; offer cooled boiled water or occasionally diluted unsweetened fruit juice at mealtimes if you want to give your baby an alternative to milk

- **tea:** can reduce iron absorption

- **low-fat and high-fiber foods:** babies need more calories and less bulk to give them the energy they need to grow

- **processed foods:** these contain too much salt.

Every baby is different

Your baby may take a couple of weeks to get the hang of solids. This is fine, as long as she is drinking plenty of milk to meet her nutritional needs.

On the other hand, your baby may race ahead and manage two or three "meals" a day in no time at all. If she is happily eating solids, coping well with taking food from a spoon, and enjoying a wide range of fruit and vegetable purées, you may wish to start gradually introducing other foods such as red meat, poultry, lentils, or split peas to her purées.

Remember that your baby's digestive system is still adjusting to solid food, so add only small quantities of new foods—and still just one at a time in case she has an allergic reaction. You may find that it takes longer for your baby to accept meat and poultry, so purée a tiny amount with her favorite vegetable.

" Not all of Rowan's food ends up in his mouth—especially when he tries to **feed himself**! But he's having such a good time, I just **don't worry** about the mess. "

STEPHANIE, mother of Rowan, seven months

4

7 to 9 months

Your baby is growing up quickly, and mealtimes are becoming a very different affair. In the next few weeks, he'll learn how to chew and will discover the fun of finger foods. Now that he can sit up on his own, you can invest in a highchair. And as the number of foods you can give your baby rapidly expands, mealtimes will become easier as he starts to enjoy some of the same foods as everyone else.

Gaining independence

Over the next few months, your baby will be building up to three regular meals a day with two or three snacks in between. While you prepare his meals, remember to keep talking to him about his food, what you are doing, and how well he is doing. Make sure you keep distractions such as television and toys well out of sight.

He'll now be sitting up on his own for extended periods, and he'll be eager to get more involved in feeding himself. Giving him his own spoon will encourage him, as will offering him finger foods. Invest in plenty of bibs and a floor mat! Playing with food—touching it, pulling it apart, throwing it—is perfectly normal.

It's best not to worry about how much ends up on the floor and how much food actually reaches his mouth. Your baby will eat when he's hungry, and your role is to keep mealtimes as happy and relaxed as possible.

Introducing more texture

The range of foods your baby can eat will gradually increase (see page 37), and you can start introducing lumpier food so he can develop his chewing skills. He'll still use his gums to chew for a while yet, so don't imagine he'll be able to cope with a steak—even if his first teeth have appeared! Instead, mash rather than purée his meals, using a fork or potato masher. Softer food that's suitable for eating with fingers, such as bread or pasta, can be left whole.

Talk to your healthcare provider if your baby does not seem to accept foods that are more textured.

(continued on page 34)

Expert tips

As your baby naturally becomes more inquisitive and active, you'll need to be extra alert and take precautions to help keep him safe.

• Always strap your baby in to his highchair—between seven and nine months is an age when he is mastering many new physical skills and may try to climb out. This is especially dangerous if he should fall with food in his mouth because he could choke.

• Don't let your baby eat anything he's already mouthed and then left lying around for an hour or so—it may give him an upset stomach.

• Always supervise your baby when he is eating or drinking— almost all children gag on some food at some stage, and you need to be close by to react quickly if this happens (see page 34).

When is the best time to start giving my baby finger foods?

Every day your baby is getting better at using his hands and fingers, and this makes it easier for him to try things such as feeding himself. His hand–eye coordination is improving by leaps and bounds, and now he can pick up a piece of food and then put it into his mouth—although not without making a bit of a mess!

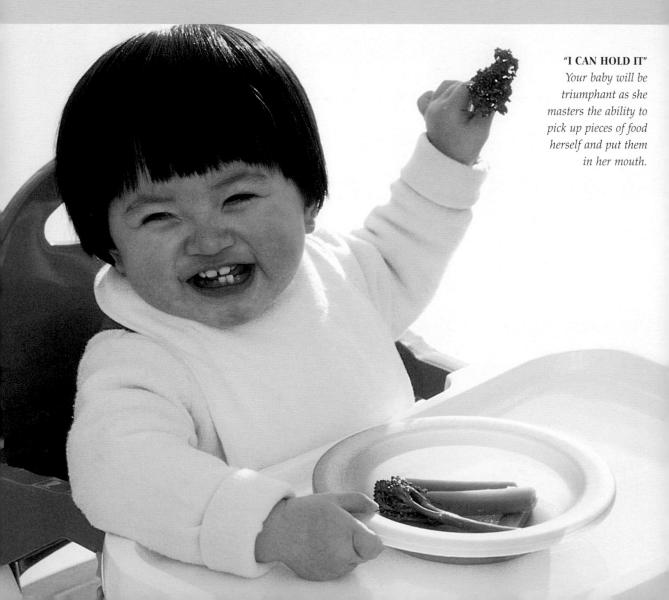

"I CAN HOLD IT"
Your baby will be triumphant as she masters the ability to pick up pieces of food herself and put them in her mouth.

Getting started

Most babies are ready for finger food by about seven months. For a while, your baby will hold the food in his fist and work hard to push in the last mouthful using the flat of his hand. Over the next few months, however, he'll start to pick up things using his thumb and forefinger, a skill called the pincer grasp. In time, this will allow him to pick up tiny pieces of food such as raisins or peas.

Your baby can easily choke from eating too fast or putting too much into his mouth. Stay close—and never leave your baby alone at mealtimes.

Learning to chew

Practicing chewing is important, and not only because it means your baby can eat a wider range of foods. Chewing also helps your baby practice moving his mouth and tongue in preparation for speech. Your baby is using his gums to chew, so choose foods that can be gummed to a soft consistency or will dissolve in his mouth without chewing. Here are some ideas:

★ cubes of bread, rice cakes, and toast
★ dry cereals
★ chunks of soft fruit, such as banana or melon
★ small pieces of cooked vegetables, such as carrots, broccoli, and cauliflower
★ well-cooked pasta, cut down in size if necessary
★ tiny cubes of hard cheese.

PREPARING FINGER FOOD
Even if your baby has some teeth, he'll still use his gums to chew for a while. Always cut food into manageable chunks, and don't offer him too much at a time. He might just try to stuff it all in at once—or sweep it all onto the floor!

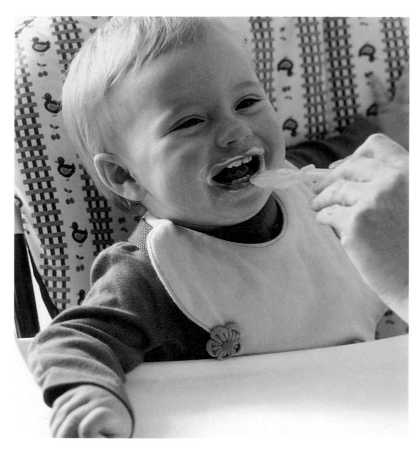

(continued from page 31)
Give your baby lots of encouragement:
- offer him a spoonful of food and say, "Mmm, doesn't this look good?"
- offer familiar foods you know he likes—he's more likely to accept a coarser texture in a food he's enjoyed before
- avoid surprises—coming across a lump in a "smooth" food, such as fruit pulp in yogurt, may be upsetting and make him suspicious of other foods
- let him snack on finger foods— offering small cubes of toast or soft fruit between meals will allow him to discover new textures at his own pace.

MAKE MEALTIMES FUN
Keeping mealtimes relaxed and simply enjoying feeding your baby will ensure they become a fun part of your routine.

Preventing choking

Introducing lumpier food and finger food brings with it the risk of choking. Children don't learn to chew and swallow efficiently until they are two or three years old. And when they are first learning to eat finger food, they may bite off a large piece and try to swallow it without chewing first. If your baby starts to gag or choke on a piece of food— or anything else—he may not be able to cough forcefully enough to dislodge it without help from you.

Minimize the risk of choking by:
- staying with him at all times while he is eating
- cutting his food into pieces small enough to swallow whole
- encouraging him to eat slowly and not gulp his food
- only letting him eat when he's sitting down—not running around or playing
- teaching him to chew and swallow first before talking or laughing
- always strapping him in to his

highchair—if he falls out with food in his mouth, he may choke
- never giving him the following:
    large pieces of raw carrot
    whole grapes
    popcorn
    uncooked peas
    celery
    hard candy
Take care also with hot dogs and other types of sausages—they should always be cut lengthwise and then into smaller pieces.

Meal ideas

- **Breakfast**

Rice cakes, well-cooked scrambled egg yolks, mashed bananas, whole-wheat toast fingers, breakfast cereal (made with whole cow's milk) with fruit purée.

- **Lunch**

Mashed vegetables and minced chicken, baked cauliflower and cheese with carrots, pasta with tomato sauce and grated cheese, boned white fish with well-cooked rice and peas.

- **Desserts**

Natural yogurt with fruit purée, pear slices (skin and seeds removed), homemade rice pudding with finely chopped dried apricots.

Choosing a highchair

A highchair will keep your baby safe and provide a seat at the right height, and you can use it between meals for your baby to sit in and play with his toys. Look for:

- sturdy construction—folding models are often the most popular, since they collapse for easy storage
- a five-point safety harness—you should always strap your baby in to his highchair, even if he'll be sitting in it for only a few minutes
- a good-sized food/play tray that's easy to clean; a deep rim will help prevent dishes and food from being pushed off, and a detachable tray will help with cleaning
- a wipe-clean, comfortably padded seat.

Questions & Answers

My baby won't eat. How can I encourage him?

There will be times when your baby either rejects his food outright or is more inclined to play with it than eat it. At this age, babies are easily distracted, so it's worth making sure mealtimes take place at quiet times of the day when you can give him your full attention. If he's only interested in playing with his food, he's probably just not hungry. It may also be the case that your baby is teething—first teeth usually make an appearance between six and nine months, and it's not unusual for babies to lose their appetite if they are suffering from teething pain or discomfort. Never force your child to eat, and avoid making mealtimes a battle. If he doesn't want any more, take his food away and try again later with something else.

We make a terrible mess every mealtime! How can I stop my baby from trying to grab the spoon from me?

Babies like to imitate, and if your baby sees you with a spoon, he'll want one too. Satisfy his need for independence by giving him his own spoon to hold, but make sure he's getting enough food by still using one yourself and slipping in mouthfuls when you can. And meanwhile, try to ignore the mess—this phase will soon pass!

My baby spits out lumps. What should I do?

If this happens, don't rush your baby—until now, he's known only how to suck, and learning to chew and cope with more lumpy food requires a very different technique. Make sure he has plenty of opportunities to practice chewing by offering him finger foods as soon as he can hold them, and keep offering him lumpy food.

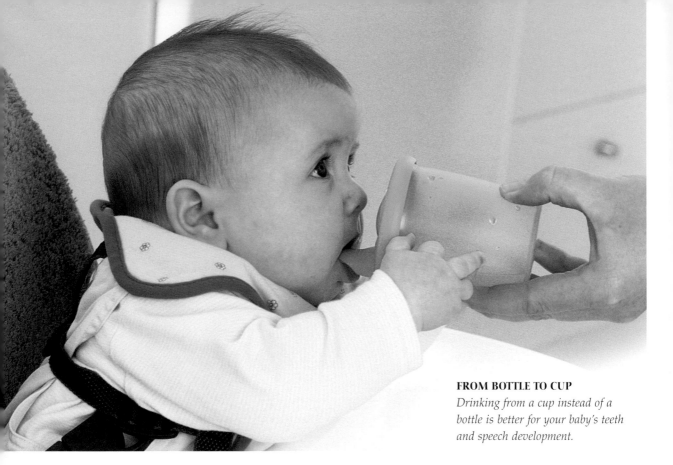

FROM BOTTLE TO CUP
Drinking from a cup instead of a bottle is better for your baby's teeth and speech development.

Foods to avoid

At this age there are still certain foods that are not suitable for your baby. Continue to avoid:

● **adding salt, sugar, and honey**: use mashed bananas for sweetening desserts instead

● **nuts**: avoid all nuts and nut products, especially if your family is known to have a history of allergies

● **foods that present a choking hazard**: these include whole grapes, nuts, large pieces of apple or raw carrots, uncooked peas, and celery

● **soft drinks**: may contain high levels of artificial sweeteners; offer cooled boiled water and occasionally diluted fruit juice at mealtimes if you want an alternative to milk

● **foods that carry a higher risk of food poisoning**, such as mold-ripened cheeses, liver pâté, and soft-boiled eggs (up to the age of nine months, only yolk should be given since this is the high-nutrition part of an egg, and whites are more likely to cause allergies)

● **low-fat and high-fiber foods**: babies need more calories and less bulk to give them the energy they need to grow

● **processed foods**: these contain too much salt.

Advancing to a cup

Your baby will naturally feel thirsty while he's eating. This is a good time to introduce a cup so he can take sips of water or fruit juice during mealtimes. Limit the amount of juice he drinks to 4 fl oz (120ml) a day and dilute it by at least one part juice to three parts water.

● Choose a nondrip, soft-spout cup for first-timers. Some babies prefer a cup with one or two handles, others prefer no handles—you may need to experiment.

● Help by holding the cup to your baby's mouth and tipping it for him to show him how it works.

Milk needs

Your baby still needs plenty of calories for energy and growth. Introducing a wider variety of food into his diet—especially protein and dairy foods—helps a lot. But to make sure your baby is getting enough protein, calcium, and vitamins, you should still give him about 17–20 fl oz (500–600ml) of formula or two full breastfeedings every day.

• Expect your baby just to play with it at first—chances are it will be waved around and thrown from the highchair. Playing with it is all part of the learning process.
• Avoid letting him carry it around with him—offer it to him only while he is in his highchair.

Extra value foods

• **Mashed bananas**
These are a high-energy food and can be easily digested. They are also full of nutrients, such as vitamins B and C, potassium, magnesium, and iodine.
• **Finely chopped meat**
Beef and lamb, in particular, are rich sources of iron and zinc.
• **Vitamin C** (in fruits and vegetables or diluted fruit juice)
Helps aid iron absorption when served at the same time as iron-rich foods.

Foods your baby can eat

Your baby is now ready for a whole range of tastes and can share many of your family meals, provided no sugar or salt has been added. Remember to introduce new tastes and textures gradually.

Try to include at least one protein-based meal a day—fish, meat, egg yolks, lentils, or beans—since these are good sources of protein and iron. Iron is particularly important—by the time your baby is six months old, the iron stores with which he was born are starting to dwindle, and milk alone will not satisfy all his daily requirements (see page 7).

Make sure your baby also has a portion each of fruit, vegetables, and starchy food every day, too. He can also eat foods containing gluten, so try white or whole-wheat bread, pasta, or couscous.

And you can now use cow's milk in meals—added to cereal, for example.

Protein
- beans and legumes
- cheese
- chicken or turkey
- cow's milk in meals (e.g., with cereal)
- eggs (yolks only, as their nutritional value is higher and they are less likely to cause allergies than whites)
- boneless fish
- red meat
- tofu

Fruit
- grapes (cut in half and seeds removed)
- oranges (seedless)
- mangoes
- melons
- tangerines (seedless)
- strawberries
- pieces of pear

Vegetables
- butternut squash
- cucumber
- green beans
- leeks
- peas
- mushrooms
- onions
- sweetcorn

Starchy food
- potatoes
- bread
- noodles
- rice
- pasta
- couscous
- breakfast cereals
- oatmeal

" Feeding Nicole is **much simpler** now. I take some potatoes, vegetables, and meat out of our main meal and mash it up for her. It's **better than ready-made** any day. "

CAROLINE, mother of Nicole, nine months

9 to 12 months

Your baby's personality is starting to shine through, and as her sense of self grows, so does her desire for independence. Over the next few months, she'll work hard at learning how to feed herself, and with your patience and praise, she'll soon master this essential skill. Meanwhile, you can enjoy her company at the table—this is a great time to start letting her join in with family meals.

Advancing skills

Your baby now has regular mealtimes with three meals—breakfast, lunch, and dinner—every day and two or three snacks as well. She can cope well with mashed or chopped food and uses finger foods to practice her chewing skills. There is now little she can't eat, so family meals can be easily adapted to feed your baby, too. Keep talking to her about what you are doing when you are preparing the meals and give her lots of praise.

Your baby's new skills make mealtimes easier:

• she can now chew, cope with different textures, and pick up shapes (talk to your healthcare provider if she has difficulties with any of these)
• her hand–eye coordination is developing fast, and learning how to feed herself is a natural step toward independence

• she's starting to recognize lots of familiar words such as "cup" and "lunchtime"
• she loves interacting with people and will enjoy social get-togethers such as mealtimes.

Introducing new tastes

Your older baby is becoming much more active—learning to crawl and then walk—which means she needs extra calories for energy and growth. She also needs a wide variety of nutrients in her diet, so now is a good time to introduce her to a broader range of foods. Since her natural inclination is to explore everything she can get her hands on, including food, this is a great age to offer your baby new tastes, although as she enjoys some independence, she is also beginning to show clear food preferences.

Extra equipment

You will find the following useful as your baby becomes more experienced at feeding herself:

• **plastic feeding bowl** with a suction pad to stop her from throwing food all over the floor

• **plastic bib** with a molded tray to catch the food that doesn't make it into her mouth

• **portable highchair** that screws or clips on to a tabletop—a great help when you are out visiting friends or relatives or on vacation.

Encouraging self-feeding

Your baby is developing a strong sense of herself in the family and of her daily routines. She'll start to look forward to mealtimes, and will recognize the cues that mean food is on the way. She'll also want to be just like you—which means feeding herself, rather than being fed by you. Encouraging your baby to self-feed means that, for a while at least, mealtimes will take longer and be messier. To begin with, your baby will probably keep turning over the spoon before it reaches her mouth. But as her finger and hand skills develop, she'll soon master the art of feeding herself.

Help her reach this milestone by:
● giving her lots of chances to practice—and ignoring the mess!
● making sure she's getting enough food in her mouth by helping her load her spoon and slipping in mouthfuls with your own spoon in between attempts
● serving her food that will stay on the spoon more easily—mashed potatoes with cheese, thick yogurts, and cottage cheese, for example
● resisting the temptation to take over—letting her struggle and succeed will boost her confidence.

Talk to your healthcare provider if your child shows no interest in self-feeding.

Getting the portions right

Every baby's appetite is different—and can change from day to day. This means it can be hard to judge how much food your baby needs. Remember that a baby's stomach can't hold very much and therefore she'll need to eat more frequently than you.

It's good to encourage your baby to eat at regular times, but accept also that she will probably need a snack between mealtimes to help fill the gaps. When she's uninterested, let her out of her highchair after 10 minutes or so and offer her another meal or snack a couple of hours later.

Teething and eating

When your baby is teething, don't be surprised if she loses her appetite. Over the next couple of months, she'll have lots of teeth coming in, and although some babies take teething in stride and show no ill effects, others become fretful and irritable.

The common signs of teething include swollen, reddened gums, excessive drooling, an inflamed cheek, a mild cough, and even a low-grade fever. Your baby will also want to bite down on anything she can get in her mouth.

If pain and discomfort affect your baby's appetite, she'll need more milk for a while. She may also refuse to drink from a cup, despite having previously loved the independence it gave her. Bottle-feeding your baby again shouldn't be a problem as long as it's only short-term.

Meanwhile, chewing and sucking on firm-textured finger food that becomes soft for easy swallowing can help soothe your baby's gums—and offer her some extra nutrition at the same time. You could also try giving her a frozen banana, for example. But never leave her alone with food in case she chokes. Commercially made teething biscuits are best avoided, since they contain a lot of sugar. Cold food—such as chilled puréed apple—may also be more appealing than warm food.

INDEPENDENT FEEDING
The time will come when your baby wants her independence. Allowing her to feed herself will boost her confidence, and she will quickly master the skills she needs.

Don't let your child carry a bottle or food around between meals or snacks (this will lessen her appetite), and a family rule of no food between meals will increase the likelihood of her eating more at mealtimes.

Planning her meals

Your baby should have at least one daily portion of fish, meat, eggs, lentils, or beans (these are the best sources of protein and iron), as well as food from the four main food groups every day. These groups are:

- dairy products such as cheese, yogurt, or full-fat cottage cheese (don't rely on just cheese for protein; use meat, fish, or egg yolks, too)
- starchy foods such as potatoes, bread, noodles, rice, pasta, and breakfast cereals
- fruits and vegetables: offer a selection of fresh fruits and vegetables so she gets used to different tastes and textures

Expert tip

Your baby can now eat the same food as you, as long as it doesn't contain added salt, sugar, or honey (see page 18). You should also avoid giving her:

- foods that carry a high risk of food poisoning (such as mold-ripened cheese, liver pâté, and soft-boiled eggs)

- whole nuts (ground nuts are fine, unless there is a history of allergies, in which case you should avoid all nuts).

When can my baby join in family meals?

Now is a great time for your baby to join in with family meals. She's a little individual with a real personality, and she enjoys having fun with everyone. Her ability to understand language is growing, and she's really trying to communicate with you. Even if she doesn't have the same food, feeding your baby when the rest of the family is eating together has lots of benefits.

A FAMILY AFFAIR
Children who regularly eat meals with the family are less likely to be fussy eaters and more likely to try a wider range of foods.

It's good to eat together

Family mealtimes are about more than just making sure everyone is getting fed—they are also social occasions and great opportunities for your baby to learn about good table manners and conversation.

Eating with your baby will also make her more adventurous when it comes to food. A baby who won't eat green beans may change her mind when she sees everyone else enjoying them.

Keep the atmosphere light and easy-going by:
★ planning family meals around your baby—if she's tired, eating together won't be fun for you or her
★ not expecting too much—if your baby turns her nose up at the food on her plate, don't take it personally; there could be various explanations for why she's not hungry today
★ ignoring the mess—have lots of paper towels handy for cleaning up as she goes.

● meat and meat alternatives such as soft, flaked white fish, well-chopped chicken or lamb, and small quantities of well-cooked lentils or beans.

Babies' appetites are very changeable, however, so check your child's diet over a week rather than a day. Talk to your healthcare provider if you think she isn't eating all the foods she needs for good nutrition.

Meal ideas

● Breakfast

Yogurt smoothie and toast, oatmeal with dried fruit, shredded wheat and milk with grated pears.

● Lunch

Lasagna, sausage and mashed potatoes and vegetables, cut-up baked potatoes with hummus/avocado/baked beans.

● Desserts

Baked bananas and full fat plain yogurt, bread-and-butter pudding, whole-wheat pancakes with fresh fruit, canned fruit in natural juice.

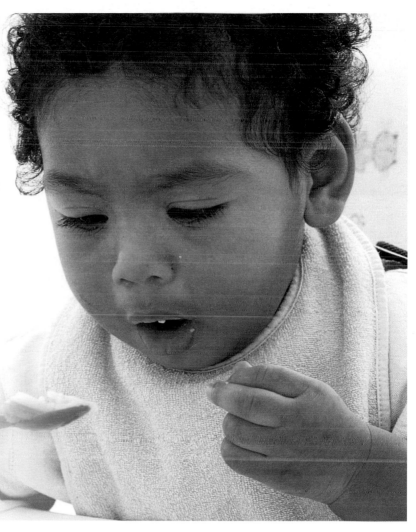

Questions & Answers

My baby is now nine months old and she still has no teeth. Should I be worried about this?

Many babies at nine months are still toothless—and some make it to their first year without a tooth in sight. Late teething doesn't have to affect your baby's move to chunkier food. Babies with and without teeth use their gums for chewing until their molars appear in the middle of the second year.

My baby doesn't seem to eat very much. Should I be encouraging her to eat more?

Your baby's stomach will fill up quickly on solid food, so when she's had enough, don't insist she has one last mouthful. This may give her an aversion to the food she's eating as well as making her feel upset and resentful. Talk to your healthcare provider if your baby:

● tries to store food in her cheeks instead of swallowing it

● refuses to accept textured food.

Tips for healthy eating

One of the best ways you can help your baby to grow up fit and healthy is to help her develop healthy eating habits now. These guidelines will help.

● **If she rejects something today, try again a few days later.**
A baby's tastes are notoriously fickle, and just because she appears not to like something now, there's no reason to assume she won't enjoy it another time. It can take 10-20 tries before a baby accepts a new food, and sometimes even more.

● **Praise her when she eats well.**
Your baby will quickly realize that healthy, natural food is good for her if you tell her what a good girl she is when she eats it.

● **Avoid "sugary" treats.**
Sugar and sugary foods contain what is termed "empty calories"—lots of sugar and energy but little nutritional value.

● **Offer healthy snacks.**
It may be easier to reach for the cookie jar when your baby is hungry between meals, but it's worth getting her used to nutritious snacks.

● **Don't allow your child to graze between meals.**
If your child sits in her highchair for a meal or snack every two to three hours, she will not be hungry in between—don't allow her to carry food or drinks around with her.

Milk needs

Your baby should still be having at least 17–20 fl oz (500–600ml) of breast milk or formula a day (this is equivalent to about two breastfeeds). Around this age, however, she may start to wean herself off the breast.

Losing interest in sucking can happen if your baby is eating lots of solids and is good at using a cup. It may, however, only be temporary. Perhaps your baby is teething. In which case sucking can put pressure on painful gums. Your baby is also curious about the world around her and she may be easily distracted if people are in the room or the television is on. Feed her in a quiet room without distractions.

Meanwhile, check that your baby is getting her full milk quota by offering her formula in her cup. If she doesn't like this, supplement her diet with plenty of full-fat yogurt and hard cheese.

- **Avoid fast food.**

Pizza, chicken nuggets, and French fries are high in fat and salt and may contain additives. If your child eats these foods regularly, she may have a greater risk of developing health problems as an adult.

Thirst quenchers

Your baby may still be resisting using a cup, but it's worth persisting with this. Drinking from a cup is better for speech development and for her teeth.

Give your baby water between meals if she seems thirsty. During the summer, when she is losing fluid through sweat, you should also offer her a drink of water a couple of times during the day. Don't make a habit of giving her juice too often— 4 fl oz (120ml) a day is plenty— because she'll love the sweeter taste and quickly refuse anything else. Too much fruit juice can cause diarrhea and diaper rash and contribute to poor dental health.

Flying food

Your baby is now much more skilled with her hands. She has mastered the pincer grasp and can pick up anything she comes across using her thumb and forefinger. This means she can guide pieces of food into her mouth more accurately—so self feeding is getting much less messy.

She's also figured out how to "let go" of things. Be prepared for lots of dropping and picking up games (she drops, you pick up). By the end of her first year she'll have discovered how to throw, too.

" I always make extra for Rashmi and then freeze it for meals the following week. This saves me time—and also makes me feel less frustrated if she doesn't eat much."

NAWSHEEN, mother of Rashmi, 11 months

" Yu-lin has always been a great eater— but at 20 months he **started refusing** everything I put in front of him. Sitting down with him and not overfilling his plate has **helped a lot. "**

JUNG, mother of Yu-lin, 20 months

One year and up

As your baby passes his first birthday, he'll become more skilled at feeding himself. He now needs to give up the bottle permanently, and you may decide it's time to stop breastfeeding, too. Over the next few months, your child will also have a surge of independence—and will love trying to get his way, especially at mealtimes!

Willful ways

Over the coming year, your child will pass many major milestones—he'll discover how to walk, for example, and may say his first words. At around 18 months, he'll also have a real drive toward independence and will want his own way whenever possible. Food inevitably becomes a battleground. Continue to involve your child in his mealtime routine by talking to him while you prepare his food, avoiding distractions such as television and toys, and making sure he's properly seated when eating.

Stress-free eating

Mealtimes with toddlers can be challenging, but most behavior—from food fads and refusing to eat to making a mess and not sitting at the table—is perfectly normal. Knowing what to expect can help a lot. So does staying unfazed. It is likely that your toddler is just exercising his will, and the less you react, the quicker he'll realize that his behavior isn't having an effect.

Now that your toddler can decide what he will and won't eat, you may worry more about his diet. Though there will be times when your cooking goes to waste, it's important to keep offering a healthy, varied diet. At this age he also needs regular snacks to keep up his energy levels.

The toddler years

As your easy-going baby turns into a challenging toddler, mealtimes can become a minefield. But it's important to realize that changing appetites, rejection of food, and food fads are all perfectly normal at this age. Even so, you may long for the days when food meant simply spooning purées into your baby's open mouth! Understanding how your child is growing and developing will help you avoid battles over food.

Happy meals

Remember to keep the atmosphere at mealtimes calm and relaxed.

Don't
- get into a fight with your toddler; losing your temper will make him more determined not to eat
- make him sit there for hours
- offer him an after-meal treat

Do
- end the meal as soon as it is obvious he won't change his mind
- remember that it won't harm him to miss a few meals
- offer him the same type of food another time if he rejects something. It may take 10–20 tries for a child to see, smell, touch, and taste foods before accepting them.

At this stage your child is:
- using up lots of energy
- developing likes and dislikes
- growing more independent
- getting easily distracted.

NO, NO, NO!
Don't worry if your child refuses to eat something—with the toddler years come surges of independence.

To help him, you can:
● offer two familiar foods with one new food
● boost his energy with healthy snacks (see below)
● accept that he won't like everything you give him, but continue to offer a wide choice so he doesn't become hooked on just a handful of foods
● help him feel as if he has some control over mealtimes by offering him food that he can easily feed himself and the chance to choose from, say, two different pieces of fruit for dessert
● sit down and eat with him whenever possible to help him enjoy his meals.

Successful mealtimes

There's little you can't give your one year old to eat, but that doesn't mean he'll love everything you put in front of him. Accept that, for a while, he'll still prefer certain tastes and textures. Try keeping to these general guidelines for mealtime success.

● **Simple cooking** Your child may dislike cooked carrots but love them raw, or he might enjoy boiled rice but not risotto. Don't worry—he'll enjoy more sophisticated food as he gets older, but for now you may have better luck keeping it plain.

● **Firm, crunchy textures** Lots of children react more strongly to texture than taste and often prefer foods that have a bit of bite—lightly steamed vegetables, for example.

● **Separate ingredients** Some children are put off if they don't know what's in their food—serving items so they are separate rather than mixed up can make all the difference.

The importance of healthy snacks

Small children tire easily without regular refueling—especially once they are up on two feet and on the move. Your baby's high energy needs can be met with a small snack between meals. You'll soon notice how quickly this revitalizes him.

It may be tempting to reach for the cookie jar, but giving him sugary snacks at this young age could encourage your baby's natural preference for sweet food as well as damaging his teeth. Offering healthy,

nutritious snacks will help your baby develop good eating habits that will last a lifetime.

Rather than having food constantly available, schedule a midmorning and afternoon snacktime into your child's

everyday routine. Here are some quick and easy ideas:
● a cracker with cream cheese
● chopped fresh raw fruit
● thin sticks of fresh raw vegetables, such as carrots and cucumber
● breadstick with hummus
● mashed bananas on toast fingers
● tiny tuna sandwiches
● peeled tangerine segments
● chopped dried fruit such as peaches.

FUN WITH FOOD
Making food look fun can help encourage your child to try out healthy options.

Stopping breastfeeding

There's no right or wrong time to give up breastfeeding—many mothers enjoy feeding their older babies, and some breastfeed and work by still giving morning and evening feedings. You may feel, however, that your baby is old enough to stop, or you may simply be ready to stop yourself. You may even be pregnant again and want to wean your first child before your second arrives.

By this age, your child should be happily drinking from a cup, even if he still enjoys the comfort of breastfeeding. This should make weaning easier—although it's still important to plan ahead and take things slowly.

• Once you have decided you want to stop, stick to your decision to avoid confusing your child.

• Be consistent start by breastfeeding only at a certain time

Caring for your child's teeth

You need to care for your baby's teeth to prevent cavities. These form when the bacteria in the mouth combine with sugar in food residues on the teeth, producing acid that attacks the tooth enamel.

• Help your child with tooth-brushing twice a day. Use a child's soft toothbrush and a pea-sized blob of toothpaste (encourage him to spit it out after brushing)

• Avoid sugary snacks, candy (see page 57), and drinks between meals.

• Before bedtime, avoid fruit juice and drinks with honey. Offer cooled boiled water instead, especially after teeth have been brushed at night.

• Dilute pure fruit juices by at least one part juice to three parts water, and give sparingly—fruit juice contains natural sugars that can cause tooth damage.

• Start taking your child to the dentist for six-month checkups. Explain beforehand what will happen, and let your child sit on your lap in the dentist's chair.

Milk needs

The amount of milk your baby is drinking at this stage will depend on him. Your older baby can drink cow's milk—although he needs a lot less milk once he is a year old: a total of 1½ cups (350ml) of whole milk per day is more than enough. If your child has too much, he will feel full and may not develop enough of an appetite for his meals.

of day (in the evening, for example) and gradually reduce the amount of time spent on the breast.

● Avoid situations where your child expects to be nursed—for example, snuggling together after lunch. Do something different instead, such as looking at a book together.

● Go together to buy a "big boy's" cup and tell him older children drink from a cup.

● When your child is tired or cranky and asks for a breastfeeding to comfort him, have a distraction ready, such as a new toy or quiet activity.

● Offer lots of kisses and cuddles.

Giving up the bottle

Now that your baby is one year old, it's much better for his teeth and health if he says goodbye to the bottle. Milk is naturally sweet and when drunk from a bottle—especially when lying down—it pools in the mouth, creating a risk of tooth decay. Also, bottle drinkers tend to eat less solid food, which may lead to eating problems later.

Some children, however, are so attached to sucking that they find it hard to accept a cup instead. You can gently get your child to give up his bottle by using some of the tips for stopping breastfeeding, as well as these ideas:

● only letting him have water in his bottle—tell him that he's a big boy now and his milk has to be drunk from a cup—this may help make the bottle less appealing

● anticipating his needs—offer drinks from a cup well before his usual time of demanding a bottle—a full stomach and quenched thirst may dampen his need for a bottle

● changing his routine—try to be out and about more in situations

Expert tip

Even though by now your child is used to firmer textures and lumpier food, he is still likely to swallow food without chewing. Don't let him run around with food in his mouth, and avoid giving him food such as whole grapes, peanuts, popcorn, whole baby tomatoes, hot dogs, uncooked peas, or hard candy.

HEALTHY FAVORITES
Fish sticks and baked beans are full of protein and iron, and a favorite with most toddlers.

where he wouldn't normally ask for a bottle and offer diverting activities that will distract him. Changing rituals attached to bottle-feeding will help him forget about it.

Popular toddler foods

Hopefully, your toddler will enjoy eating a wide range of healthy foods, but don't worry too much if at times he isn't interested. Here are some popular toddler meals that are also healthy:

• cheese on whole-wheat toast offers lots of fiber and calcium
• a baked potato filled with tuna is a complete balanced meal in itself
• good-quality fish sticks are packed with protein and contain some iron
• baked beans are a good source of iron and protein: choose a reduced sugar and salt variety
• a broiled 100 percent meat burger in a soft bread roll with salad makes a healthy, iron-packed meal.

Feeding your vegetarian baby

If you and your family are vegetarian, there is no reason why your baby shouldn't be, too. It's important that he has a good supply of protein and iron: after six months, he can eat well-cooked egg yolks, beans, and lentils. It may also be a good idea to talk to your healthcare provider about iron supplements. If you are also excluding eggs and dairy produce from your baby's diet, he may need supplements of vitamins B12 and D as well as riboflavin and calcium. Consult a registered dietician to make sure he gets adequate nutrients for healthy development.

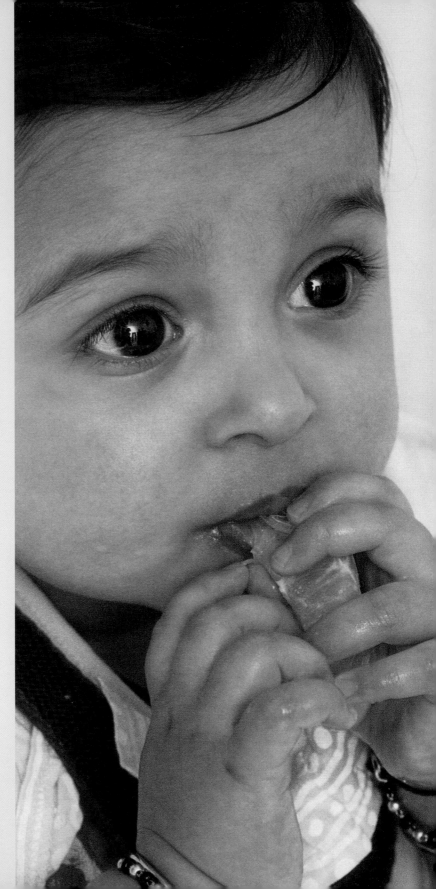

" We're really into food in our family— I love cooking, and Ayesha **enjoys helping.** She won't always eat what we make together, but she's more **likely to try it,** which is a step in the right direction. "

RAZNA, mother of Ayesha, 12 months

7

Happy, healthy eating

Making sure your child has a balanced diet is easy if you follow a few simple guidelines. Helping her enjoy mealtimes and offering her fresh, wholesome food from the start will encourage her to develop healthy eating habits that will do her good not only now but in the future, too.

Healthy habits

Feeding children can be a great chance to overhaul the whole family's diet. After all, your child is more likely to enjoy fresh, wholesome food if she sees you enthusiastically enjoying the same meal. And similarly, if you find it hard to resist a chocolate chip cookie with your morning cup of coffee, your little one will be less than impressed when she's offered a plate of vegetable sticks to snack on! If your child is brought up to think that eating healthy food is the norm, it's more likely to become a lifelong habit.

Understanding what makes a healthy diet for your child is simpler than you may think. In fact, in many ways, the guidelines are similar to those for healthy adult eating—avoid too much salt, fat, and sugar, limit the amount of processed food, and eat lots of fresh fruit and vegetables.

Monitoring what your child eats could be good for you, too!

With active, growing children, however, it's important to remember that they need more calories to keep them going and lots of protein to help them grow. So starchy food— bread, pasta, rice, and so on—has to play a major role, closely followed by meat and meat alternatives. And while low-fat, high-fiber diets may be good for grownups, they can be harmful for children.

What makes a balanced diet?

Making sure your child has a good, healthy diet isn't complicated. You don't even need to understand a lot about vitamins and minerals. The key is to offer variety. As long as you encourage your child to eat a wide range of foods in roughly the right proportions, she'll get all the nutrients she needs for healthy growth and development.

- Carbohydrates (bread, pasta, cereals, rice, couscous)

These are the best source of energy for growing children and should make up 50-60 percent of their diet by age five. Offer one serving at every meal.

- **Fruits and vegetables**

You can use fresh, frozen, canned, or dried varieties of these.

(continued on page 56)

Expert tips

- Avoid foods that are high in saturated (mostly animal) fats and have additional sugar and salt.

- Steam, bake, broil, or boil foods instead of frying or roasting them.

- Use as many fresh ingredients as possible.

- Give your child water or diluted fruit juice when she is thirsty.

- Offer raw vegetables (carrot, celery, or cucumber sticks), fruit, or bread as snacks.

What are food allergies and intolerances?

Occasionally, some babies have a bad reaction to certain foods. This can be caused by either a food allergy or a food intolerance. Your baby is more likely to develop a food allergy if you or your partner suffer from allergies—but she will probably grow out of it. A food intolerance, on the other hand, means your baby will need to avoid certain foods permanently.

Food allergies

If your baby develops a food allergy, her body is reacting to a normally harmless substance and mistaking it for a dangerous one. The immune system kicks in, producing antibodies that trigger the release of histamine. This causes allergic symptoms such as a runny nose, itchy eyes, diarrhea, or a rash. In severe cases, anaphylaxis occurs; this life-threatening condition causes swelling in the mouth and throat and difficulty in breathing. Symptoms may appear within a few minutes or up to two hours after eating. Thankfully, this is quite rare.

Nearly half of those children who develop a food allergy before they are three years old grow out of it by the age of seven.

Food intolerances

This is a nonallergic reaction to a food or additive. There are two common types of intolerance.

★ Lactose intolerance, which means a child can't digest the natural sugar in milk and milk products such as cheese and yogurt. Symptoms include stomach cramps, bloating, flatulence, and diarrhea. Lactose-free milk and dairy-free alternatives to milk, such as calcium-enriched soy drinks, are available.

★ Gluten intolerance (see page 28), which is caused by the protein found in certain grains, such as wheat, barley, rye, and perhaps oats. This can trigger celiac disease in a small number of babies. Gluten should not be given to any baby before six months of age. Once gluten intolerance has been diagnosed, foods made with grains containing gluten—such as pasta, cereals, and bread—have to be permanently avoided.

If gluten is being taken out of your child's diet on a permanent basis, it is advisable to ask your healthcare provider for an appointment to see a registered dietician to be sure her diet is adequately balanced for normal growth and development.

Some supermarkets now stock a range of products that are gluten-free, including bread, cookies, cereal, and pasta.

TROUBLESOME FOODS
Eggs, nuts, and soft-berry fruits such as strawberries are each linked to allergies in children, and bread contains gluten, which can result in intolerance if given to your child too soon.

Ways to help avoid allergies

• Breastfeed for as long as possible—and, if there are allergies in the family, avoid eating potential triggers while breastfeeding. Avoiding foods that have commonly been implicated in allergies, such as cow's milk protein, eggs, nuts, wheat, and shellfish, may help. If you feel your diet is limited, speak to your healthcare provider or ask for a referral to a registered dietician.

• Do not start weaning your baby before she is six months old.

• Delay giving your baby foods that may trigger a reaction (cow's milk, eggs, wheat, shellfish, and soft-berry fruits such as strawberries) until she is at least one year old if there is a history of allergies in the family. If there are several foods being avoided, it is advisable to ask your doctor for an appointment to see a registered dietician to help assess the diet and make sure it's providing all the nutrients your baby needs.

• Avoid nuts, especially peanuts, until your child is three years old.

• When introducing these foods—and any other new food—do so gradually and one at a time, looking out for any reactions as you go.

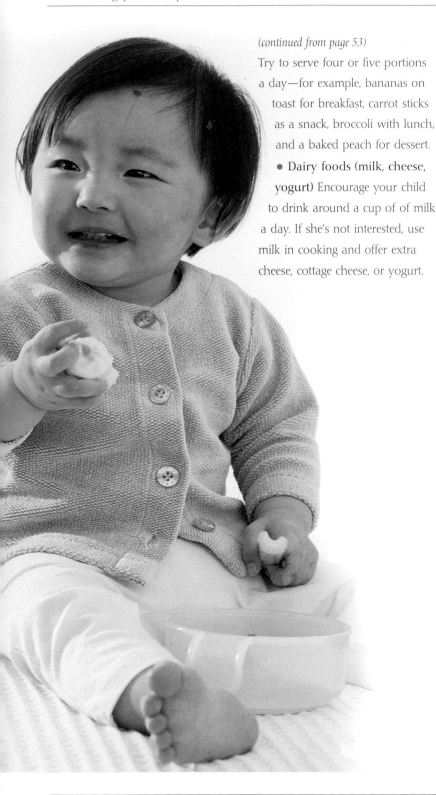

(continued from page 53)
Try to serve four or five portions a day—for example, bananas on toast for breakfast, carrot sticks as a snack, broccoli with lunch, and a baked peach for dessert.

● **Dairy foods (milk, cheese, yogurt)** Encourage your child to drink around a cup of of milk a day. If she's not interested, use milk in cooking and offer extra cheese, cottage cheese, or yogurt.

● **Meat, fish, and meat alternatives** Remember to include oily fish, such as salmon, mackerel, sardines, and pilchards, as well as white fish. These are essential sources of protein and iron. Lentils and beans are good meat alternatives, but keep the portions small.

Extra value foods

Some foods within the four main food groups have special value.

● Breakfast cereals, if fortified, are a good source of iron and vitamins.

● Lean red meat is great for minerals, iron, and zinc. Offer once or twice a week, and broil rather than fry.

● Canned sardines have lots of iron, calcium, and essential omega-3 fatty acids. Serve on toast for a tasty meal.

● Broccoli is a rich source of vitamin C, beta carotene, and fiber.

● Milk can't be beat for calcium, as well as vitamin A, riboflavin, and zinc.

● Cheddar cheese is a versatile source of protein, calcium, and calories—use in sauces, in sandwiches, on toast, or just as chunks for nibbling on.

● Bananas are energy-giving, easy to eat, and packed with potassium.

Nutritional know-how

Here are some tips to help your child get the most out of her diet.

● Offer whole-milk dairy products— children need a calorie-dense diet so keep low-fat yogurts and cheese, for example, for adults only. You can offer reduced fat milk after the age of two and skim milk after five.

• Avoid fiber-rich foods in large quantities—as long as your child has a portion a day of fruits and vegetables, she'll be getting all the fiber she needs. Too much can cause food to move too quickly through her system, not allowing enough time for nutrients to be absorbed.

• Encourage iron absorption by offering foods with vitamin C at the same time—broccoli and baked potato with homemade lamb meatballs, for example.

• As long as your child is getting the right number of daily servings from the various food groups, she will be getting plenty of the vitamins and minerals she needs and won't need expensive supplements.

Fussy eaters

Why are some children more fussy about their food than others? There are a number of different reasons. Some children, for example, are wary of new experiences—and approach new foods cautiously. Some are unusually sensitive to certain tastes and textures. Others learn early in their lives that they can use food to manipulate their parents and attract attention.

The food guide pyramid

The two most important food groups in your baby's diet are carbohydrates and fruits and vegetables. Next are protein-rich foods such as meat, legumes, and dairy products. Sugars, fats, and oils should form the smallest part (the amounts that occur naturally in other foods will be more than enough).

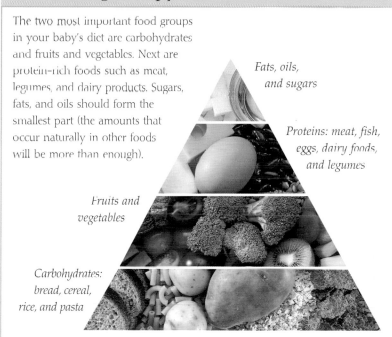

Fats, oils, and sugars

Proteins: meat, fish, eggs, dairy foods, and legumes

Fruits and vegetables

Carbohydrates: bread, cereal, rice, and pasta

Understanding your child's needs will help create happy mealtimes. It's not worth trying to feed her when she is overtired, for example—little ones especially lose interest in food when they are ready to sleep. Slow eaters need plenty of time to finish their meal, and many fussy eaters respond well to being offered a choice—two types of vegetables, perhaps.

Avoiding conflict

It's important to stay as calm and as neutral as possible at mealtimes. Help keep the atmosphere happy with a few simple strategies.

Candy

Candy not only fills your child up on empty calories, but can also damage her teeth. It would be impossible to ban candy completely, but you could:

• nominate a "candy day"—one day a week when your child can have a portion of candy

• avoid chewy candy if possible—opt for chocolate instead

• encourage your child to eat her portion of candy all at once—the impact on her teeth will be less if it is eaten all at once instead of spread out over the day.

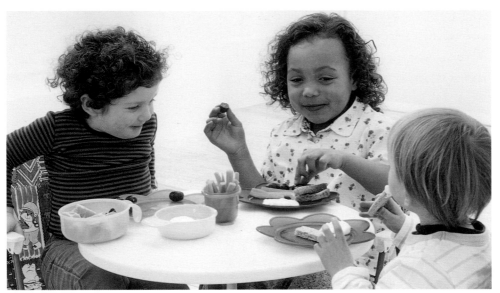

TEA PARTIES
*Inviting your child's
friends to tea—
let her choose what
to serve—can be an
enjoyable occasion
for everyone.*

• Use some gentle persuasion—
you should never force your child
to eat, but if she is not eating
simply because she is in a bad
mood, tired, or distracted, then
some kind encouragement can help.
Most children will try a few mouthfuls
because they know this isn't the
same as having to clear the plate.
Using food as a bribe ("If you don't
finish your vegetables, you can't
have any dessert!") or a reward is
not successful in the long run—it
teaches a child that food can be a
powerful weapon when it comes to
getting what they do or don't want.

• Know when to compromise—rather
than removing the whole plate of food,
try to find some middle ground. If she
won't eat her meatloaf, for example,
say, "That's fine, but you can eat
your green beans, can't you?"
• Give in gracefully—there will
always be times when your child
just won't be persuaded to eat, in
which case it's better to accept this
without a fuss. Children's likes and
dislikes change all the time, so tell
her, "I know you don't like this
today—but you may next week."

Lots of children grow out of being
fussy eaters. Eating with friends,
for example, often encourages them
to be more adventurous. And
children who fuss for attention often
give up when they don't get the
response they are looking for.

Eating out

Being prepared will allow eating out
to be a fun occasion for all members
of your family. Explain to your child
what to expect and she will more
than likely rise to the occasion.

• Time your outing carefully—if
your child is tired or very hungry,
she is less likely to cope well.

• Choose a child-friendly place—
lots of restaurants provide highchairs
or booster seats, crayons and paper,
and a special children's menu.

• Take your own distractions—a
favorite book or selection of small
toys will help keep your child
amused while she's waiting for her
food or when she's finished.

• Order her favorites—your child
will enjoy her meal more if she's
served things she likes.

The best approach to challenging behavior or unreasonable demands is to ignore them or quietly and quickly end the meal.

Eating together

Eating together as a family is one of the best ways of encouraging your child to enjoy her food. Talking at the table gives your child a chance to practice her social skills, and watching how you behave will help lay the foundations for good table manners. Try:

• eating together as often as possible, or at least sitting with your children while they have lunch or supper

• getting your child involved—she can help set the table or take a dish to the dining room—to help her enjoy the sense of occasion

• avoiding arguments—mealtimes should provide an opportunity for everyone to relax and enjoy each other's company

• encouraging your child to join in the conversation—ask specific questions, such as "Did you play with your best friend today?"

• not expecting too much—small children don't have the patience to sit at the table for long, so once your child has finished her food, let her leave the table.

Encouraging healthy mealtimes

• Provide a regular routine for sit-down meals and snacks.

• Enthuse about fresh, wholesome food—"Mmm...this fruit salad is so delicious!"

• Cook one healthy meal for everyone—don't offer alternatives.

• Offer as much choice as possible. If you cook four vegetables, your child might eat two of them.

• Praise her when she eats well.

• Don't give up—your child may not be interested in sweet potatoes today, but she may try them next week.

Weaning your baby

Helping your baby move from a milk diet to family food is simple if you follow these general guidelines. Bear in mind that if there is a family history of allergies, introduction of certain foods should be delayed (see page 55).

Baby's age	Type of food	Milk and dairy products
6 months	Start with a fine semi-liquid purée mixed with breast milk, formula, or cooled boiled water, thickening it over the next few weeks.	Your baby still needs at least 20 fl oz (600ml) breast milk or formula a day.
7–9 months	Mashed or chopped; finger foods, when your baby can hold things.	Your baby still needs at least 17–20 fl oz (500–600ml) breast milk or formula a day; small cubes of cheddar cheese or cottage cheese; you can now use cow's milk to mix food or add to breakfast cereals.
9–12 months	Most foods should now be mashed or chopped, and some left whole for your baby to chew on.	Your baby still needs at least 17–20 fl oz (500–600ml) breast milk or formula a day; whole-milk yogurts are fine, but choose unsweetened ones and add fruit.
One year and up	Your child can now eat most family food as along as it's cut up for her and doesn't contain added salt or sugar. You can now safely introduce honey to her diet.	Encourage your child to have 12 fl oz (350ml) milk a day; whole cow's milk is now fine as a main drink.

Starchy food	Vegetables and fruit	Meat and meat alternatives
Baby rice cereal	Puréed cooked carrots, parsnips, zucchini, rutabagas, sweet potatoes, or broccoli. Puréed stewed apples or pears, mashed bananas.	Once solids are established, you can start to introduce a small amount of puréed, lean, soft-cooked beef, lamb, pork, or poultry, or puréed lentils or split peas.
Try white or whole-wheat bread, pasta, rice, noodles, couscous, oatmeal, and other breakfast cereals.	Cucumber, green beans, leeks, peas, mushrooms, onions, sweetcorn, tomatoes. Citrus fruits (seedless), grapes (seedless, cut in half), mango, melon, strawberries.	Introduce a little boneless white fish (cod or haddock), hard-boiled egg yolk (no egg white until nine months), mashed, well-cooked beans and legumes.
Homemade pizza, french fries, cakes, puddings, and cookies are healthier alternatives to store-bought versions, which are high in fat, salt, and sugar.	Encourage your baby to eat raw fruit and lightly cooked vegetables as snacks; canned fruit in natural juice is a healthy alternative to fresh fruit.	Meat and meat alternatives: sliced ham, chicken, or turkey, and small chopped sausages make good finger foods, introduce boiled eggs or omelets.
Offer one serving of potato, pasta, bread, rice, or couscous at every meal; limit very starchy food such as pastries, chips, or other salty snacks.	Try to serve four small portions a day—offer as snacks or blend into a stew or soup. Do not include nuts in your child's diet until she is at least three years old (see page 55).	Start to include oily fish such as salmon, mackerel, sardines, and pilchards; trim the fat off meat and skin chicken before serving; carefully remove small bones from fish.

Useful contacts

UNITED STATES

American Academy of Pediatrics
(847) 434-4000
www.aap.org
Educational brochures and fact sheets on children's health

American Association for Premature Infants
(513) 956-4331
www.appi-online.org
Support and information for parents of premature infants

American Dietetic Association
(800) 877-1600
www.eatright.org
The largest US organization of food and nutrition professionals

Bright Futures
Georgetown University
(202) 784-9556
www.brightfutures.org
Provides education and training for healthy mothers and babies

Cleft Palate Foundation
(800) 24-CLEFT (242-5338)
www.cleftline.org
Support for parents of children with cleft palates

Food and Nutrition Information Center
Agricultural Research Service, USDA
(301) 504-5719
www.nal.usda.gov/fnic
USDA source for current and reliable nutrition information

La Leche League International
(800) LA-LECHE (525-3243)
www.lalecheleague.org
International organization offering advice and information on breastfeeding

Maternal and Child Health Bureau
(301) 443-2170
mchb.hrsa.gov
Provides leadership to improve access to healthcare for mothers and children

Mothers of Supertwins
(516) 434-6678
www.mostonline.org
Support and information for mothers of multiples

National Healthy Mothers, Healthy Babies Coalition
(703) 836-6110
www.hmhb.org
Coalition promoting optimal health for mothers and babies

National Institute of Child Health and Human Development
(800) 370-2943
www.nichd.nih.gov
Promotes child health through research and public information

Nutrition for Kids
www.nutritionforkids.com
Information on nutrition for children of all ages

Nutrition.Gov
www.nutrition.gov
Broad range of nutrition information from the US government

The Vegetarian Resource Group (VRG)
(410) 366-VEGE (366-8343)
www.vrg.org
Includes information on vegetarian diets for infants

CANADA

Canadian Institute of Child Health
(613) 230-8838
www.cich.ca
A national charitable organization dedicated to improving and protecting the health of children and youth in Canada

Canadian Paediatric Society
(613) 526-9397
www.cps.ca
Promotes quality healthcare for all Canadian children

La Leche League of Canada
Breastfeeding Referral Service
(800) 665-4324
www.lalecheleaguecanada.ca
Help and support for women who are breastfeeding

National Institute of Nutrition
(613) 235-7032
www.nin.ca
Provides nutrition advice for children and links to other food and health-related resources

Parent Help Line
Kids Help Phone National Office
(416) 586-5437
www.parentsinfo.sympatico.ca
Offers support and advice on parenting concerns, including eating and mealtimes

Index

A

age
    under 6 months 7, 8
    around 6 months 16-19, 23 29, 60-61
    7-9 months 31-37, 60-61
    9-12 months 39-45, 60-61
    12 months plus 47-51, 60-61
allergies 8, 11, 55
    food allergies and intolerances 23, 24, 28, 29, 54-55
appetite and hunger 8, 18, 26, 40, 43

B

baby rice cereal 14, 18, 19
balanced diet 37, 41-45, 51, 53-57, 60-61
behaving badly 47-48, 57-59
breast- and bottle-feeding 7, 8, 11, 19, 49-50, 55
    see also milk needs

C

calorie requirements 7, 29, 36, 37, 39, 53
candy 57
carbohydrates (starchy foods) 37, 41, 53, 57, 61
celiac disease 28, 54
cereals 14, 18, 19, 26
chewing and gumming 31, 33, 39, 43
choking 17, 19, 31, 33, 34
commercial baby food 27-29, 40
constipation 26
crying 26
cups 36-37, 40, 45, 50

D

dairy foods 41, 56, 57, 60
diaper changes 19
diarrhea 26
digestive system 7, 8, 11, 19, 29
drinks 29, 36, 45, 49, 50

E

eating between meals 41, 44
eating out 58
encouragement 16, 27, 34, 35, 40, 44
equipment 13, 39

F

family meals 27, 42, 59
fast foods 45
feeding techniques 16-18, 36 37, 40
fiber 29, 36, 57
finger foods 31, 32-33, 34, 40
first feed 13-19
fish 56
food allergies and intolerances 23, 24, 28, 29, 54-55
food combinations 24-25
food hygiene 21, 29, 31
food poisoning 21, 29, 41
food preparation 20-21, 33, 48, 53
food pyramid 57
food rejection and refusal 17, 18, 19, 35, 43, 44, 47-48
foods to avoid 18-19, 29, 34, 36, 41
freezing and storing 21
fruits and vegetables 29, 37, 41, 53, 56, 57, 61
    purées 15, 20-21, 24, 26
fussy eaters 42, 57-8

G

gagging 17, 31
gluten 28, 54
grazing 41, 44
gumming and chewing 31, 33, 39, 43

H

hand-eye coordination 7, 32, 39
head control 7, 8, 10
healthy eating 37, 41-45, 51, 53-57, 60-61

highchairs 31, 35, 39
honey 18, 29, 36
hunger and appetite 8, 18, 26, 40, 43

I

immune system 11, 24, 54
independence 7, 31, 39, 40, 47
iron 7, 14, 15, 37, 57

L

lactose intolerance 54
lumps 34, 35

M

meals
    around 6 months 23
    7-9 months 31, 35
    9-12 months 39, 40-43
    12 months plus 47, 48, 51, 57-59
meat and meat alternatives 37, 41, 43, 56, 61
milk needs 9-10, 25, 26, 37, 40, 45, 50

N

nutritional requirements 7, 9, 25, 37, 39
nuts and nut products 29, 36, 41

O

organic foods 29

P

pincer grasp 33, 45
premature babies 9
preparing food 20-21, 33, 48, 53
processed foods 29, 36
protein 37, 41, 43, 53, 56, 57, 61
purées 15, 20-21, 23-24, 26

R

reactions to new tastes 17, 18, 25, 44
routine, mealtime 23, 40, 47

S

safety 17, 31, 34, 51
salt 18, 27, 29, 36
seating 13, 24, 31, 35, 39
self-feeding 40, 45
sleep 19
smell 10-11
snacks 40, 41, 44, 47, 48, 53
spitting out food 35
spoons and spoon feeding 13, 16, 18, 27, 31, 40
starchy foods 37, 41, 53, 57, 61
    baby cereals 14, 18, 19, 26
stomach complaints 26
stools 19
store-bought baby food 27-29
storing and freezing 21
sucking 18, 25, 26
sugar 18, 27, 29, 36, 44
swallowing 7, 26, 34

T

taste 10, 14-15
    baby's reactions 17, 18, 25
    introducing new tastes 18, 23-25, 26, 29, 37, 44
teething 35, 40
texture 11, 15, 31, 34, 48
toddlers 47-51
tongue-thrust reflex 7, 8, 17
tooth care 49, 50
touch 11

V

vegetables see fruits and vegetables
vegetarians 51

W

weaning 49-50, 60-61

Acknowledgments

Dorling Kindersley would like to thank Sally Smallwood and Ruth Jenkinson for the photography, Sue Bosanko for compiling the index, and Alyson Lacewing for the proofreading. Thanks also to Tanya Carr (consultant).

Models

Ilaria Pesci, Cecilia Woodhouse with Joshua, Sylvia Davidson, Kim with Carla Rabin, Keith with Anthony Blackmore, Anne with Freddie Dowland, Julia Harris and Colin with Mia Short, Tristan Smith, Jonathan Ballejo, Wendy with Jenny Cheng, Doug with Gil Krikler, Elena Marrai, Theo Angeli, Madalena Grigoletti, Avni and Alkesh with Dhanvi Shah, Dylan Ramirez, Corinna with Hannah Hyman, Lorna Zheng, Jeffrey Jaramillo, Taylor Smith, Sydney Barron, Chukwuma Orji, Phoebe Berman, Angel Kennett-Smith, Lulu with Paul and Eleanor Manitaras, Paul Bradley

Hair and makeup Louise Heywood, Victoria Barnes, Susie Kennett, Amanda Clarke

Picture researcher Anna Bedewell

Picture librarian Romaine Werblow

Picture credits Dorling Kindersley would like to thank the following for their kind permission to reproduce their photographs:
(abbreviations key: t=top, b=bottom, r=right, l=left, c=center)
40: Science Photo Library: Mark Clarke (bl).

All other images © Dorling Kindersley. For further information, see www.dkimages.com